THE PUBLIC SCHOOLS

AND SPIRITUAL VALUES

THE JOHN DEWEY SOCIETY

MEMBERSHIP OF THE YEARBOOK COMMITTEE

JOHN S. BRUBACHER, *Editor*
Associate Professor of Education
Yale University

SAMUEL M. BROWNELL
Professor of Education
Yale University

JOHN L. CHILDS
Professor of Education
Columbia University

RUTH CUNNINGHAM
Secretary of the Department of
Supervision and Curriculum Development
National Education Association

WILLIAM H. KILPATRICK
Professor Emeritus of Education
Columbia University

MARION Y. OSTRANDER
Associate Professor of Education
Adelphi College

WILLIAM J. SANDERS
Professor of Education
New Haven State Teachers College

A. L. THRELKELD
Superintendent of Public Schools
Montclair, New Jersey

THE
PUBLIC SCHOOLS
AND
SPIRITUAL VALUES

WRITTEN IN COLLABORATION

BY

JOHN S. BRUBACHER

EDITOR

SAMUEL M. BROWNELL   WILLIAM H. KILPATRICK
JOHN L. CHILDS   MARION Y. OSTRANDER
RUTH CUNNINGHAM   WILLIAM J. SANDERS
A. L. THRELKELD

HARPER & BROTHERS PUBLISHERS

NEW YORK AND LONDON

THE PUBLIC SCHOOLS AND SPIRITUAL VALUES

This book is complete and unabridged
in contents, and is manufactured in strict
conformity with Government regulations
for saving paper.

12317

CONTENTS

PREFACE

The Second World War, far more than the First, has been a crisis in spiritual values. In a life-and-death struggle over spiritual values it is necessary to mobilize every resource both for the winning of the war and no less for the winning and maintenance of a just peace. Not least among these resources should be the public school. Society should be able to depend upon its schools above any other agency to inspire youth with the abiding loyalties necessary to carry it through the trials of war and through the perhaps even greater trials of peace.

Yet, at this critical moment in which our spiritual values stand in dire need of support from the public school, doubt seems to have arisen in a portion of the public mind whether the school is fulfilling—or even can fulfill—this social function. The stumblingblock leading to doubt seems to center on the conception of "spiritual" values. The term "spiritual" is frequently, if not commonly, associated with religion. By long tradition religion is barred from our public school curriculum. Therefore, a portion of the public reasons, the public school is not supposed to nor able to teach spiritual values. Even worse, these people infer its refraining from teaching spiritual values is partially responsible for the jeopardy in which our spiritual values are now placed.

This logic was examined at a meeting of the executive board of the John Dewey Society in the spring of 1943. After due deliberation, it seemed to the board and their advisers that the public school does in fact and as a matter of duty should teach spiritual values. This positive conviction seemed moreover so important to them that they decided to devote one of the Society's yearbooks to its exposition.

Thereupon the board proceeded to the discussion of a suitable membership to compose a committee for such a yearbook. At once it became apparent that the character of the membership would depend to a large extent on the kind of yearbook to be undertaken. Should it be one in which the committee would endeavor to set forth a point of view that would be common and acceptable to as large a number of the public as possible? Or should it frankly and avowedly accept some particular point of view, like secularism or supernaturalism, and crusade in behalf of that as the most promising long-run policy? To follow the latter policy might guarantee a cutting edge and integration of viewpoint, but it guaranteed almost as surely the alienation of large numbers of supporters of public schools. To seek a premise that would invite the largest possible support for the public school might risk the statement of inoffensive and tepid generalities. But it also would give the best earnest of a point of view which could be the basis of immediate action during and after this war crisis in spiritual values.

The board decided upon the first alternative, a yearbook which would seek as much unity of action and opinion as it was possible to get under present circumstances. It considered the possible racial, religious, and professional interests that should be represented in such a yearbook committee. Difficulties at once presented themselves. Since the yearbook was to aim at a statement promising a maximum of agreement, it seemed desirable to select committee members for more than their outstanding advocacy of a particular point of view. It seemed desirable to pick them also for their ability to co-operate with people of opposite views. To find members possessing this rare combination of qualities was not always easy. Those desired were not always available. Selection was further complicated by the war and the difficulties of transportation. Hence, it became necessary to select people within a limited radius so that meetings of the committee might be held with as little tax on public transportation as possible.

The present yearbook committee was finally composed of the following members: Samuel M. Brownell, Professor of Education at Yale University; John L. Childs, Professor of Education at Columbia University; Ruth Cunningham, Secretary of the Department of Supervision and Curriculum Development, National Education Association; William H. Kilpatrick, Professor Emeritus of Education at Columbia University; Professor Marion Y. Ostrander of Adelphi College; William J. Sanders, Professor of Education in the New Haven State Teachers College; A. L. Threlkeld, Superintendent of Public Schools, Montclair, N.J.; and John S. Brubacher, Associate Professor of Education at Yale University, serving as chairman.

The initial plan of the yearbook, as already stated, was to make a statement about public schools and spiritual values which would win a maximum of support from both the laity and the educational profession. On the whole this plan was achieved. The first three and the last four chapters are a minimum statement in which each one on the yearbook committee finds himself in agreement. Each might wish at points to add more but that more would probably cause division of opinion among the committee.

For a while it was the thought of the committee to close the book at the point where differences set in. But the more they thought about stopping there, the more it seemed desirable to do more. As much common support as the first three and last four chapters represented, there was no doubt more that could be said on behalf of teaching spiritual values in the public schools. Why not indicate these other supporting arguments, though controversial and though only limited numbers would rally to them? And why not let each side know and understand the other's position better? The advantages of such an extension appearing to outweigh its disadvantages, two further chapters, Chapters IV and V, were agreed upon. One was planned to indicate the manner in which a secularist would wish to supplement the common statement and the other the manner in which a supernaturalist would wish to supplement it.

Except for these two chapters the yearbook committee has tried to write this book as a joint enterprise. In the first instance, each chapter was assigned to some member for an initial draft. This draft was later subjected to criticism of the whole committee. In an important sense, therefore, the first three and last four chapters are the joint opinion of the whole committee. In some cases redrafts were criticized and redrafted again and again till they met the approval of the entire committee. Indeed, even Chapters IV and V came in for their share of criticism although naturally less pressure was brought to bear on their respective authors to make statements agreeable to the rest of the committee. Because of this joint nature of the yearbook enterprise, the authorship of individual chapters is not credited to specific members of the committee except in the case of Chapters IV and V. Chapter IV was written by Professor Childs and Chapter V by Professor Sanders. Perhaps the absence of individual names will help to reinforce the notion that spiritual values are and can be taught in a public school whose clientele is composed of people of diverse philosophies and religions.

THE PUBLIC SCHOOLS

AND SPIRITUAL VALUES

Chapter I

INTRODUCTION

THE need to support and defend spiritual values is most seriously urgent upon the world today. Our times are troubled and we in them. Science and its offspring, rapid change, have so upset many long-existing customs and beliefs and thus brought such difficult social problems that many among us stand uneasy and fearful, perplexed as to what to think, what to believe, what standards to uphold, what values to seek. Meanwhile, an inadequate economic outlook had too much enthroned individualistic selfishness and a calculating disregard of the common good. On top of all this, a selfish aggressive war threatened civilization by seeking to overthrow democracy and enthrone despotism. With civilization thus assailed within and without we find many people losing their faith in human effort, questioning man's ability to manage the world his science has produced. It is this total situation of callous selfishness, undigested social change, disturbed culture, weakened authority of custom, social perplexity —with the resulting lessening of man's faith in himself—it is this situation which calls so urgently upon us to uphold and strengthen our spiritual values. Indeed the essential quality of civilization itself seems herein at stake.

The particular concern of this book is the public school and the part it can and should play in the support and defense of the spiritual values necessary to a desirable civilization.

If our democracy is to prosper, it must be in the quality of the people themselves; for these both effect and constitute such a prosperity. It is to this end that the public school exists. Its peculiar duty and opportunity is to work with the young of all the people, along all feasible lines of consciously directed educational effort, to nurture them to effective life and citizenship. As over against the loss of faith, the perplexity, the spiritual unrest of many older people, the public school must upbuild in the young the spiritual values needed for a just and wholesome civilization. Instead of division and conflict, it must build unity. In place of doubt and fear it must build faith, faith in right and good, faith that effort wisely directed can in the long run prevail at least reasonably against the troubles that assail. Such a public service we of this book count the chief task and aim of the public school. It is to help the public school discharge this particular spiritual task and duty that this book has been undertaken.

That certain spiritual values are necessary to any proper civilization we count beyond question. Man cannot live by bread alone, more is essential. And no man liveth to himself; man as more than mere animal is inherently social and must live in company. Moreover, man has, since his first appearance on earth, perhaps a million years ago, been selectively accumulating, very, very slowly at first but more rapidly in recent times, all those human contrivances and discoveries whereby he might the better exploit his varied resources, both inner and outer, to more satisfactory living. This accumulation, the culture we call it, consists chiefly of language, tools, customs, knowledge, institutions, distinctions, standards. Each group lives its culture and the result is its civilization. No civilization, however, could we of this book approve which does not embody and make manifest certain essential spiritual values: moral insight, integrity of thought and act; equal regard for human personality wherever found; faith in the free play of intelligence both to guide study and to direct action; and, finally, those further values of refined thought and feeling requisite to bring life to its finest quality. These essential spiritual values are not born in us; they come to each individual only as he constructively acquires them from his youth up; and it is to this end that the school mainly exists.

As we thus desire to help the public school discharge its duty of teaching these needed spiritual values, certain objectors come forward to deny either the right or the possibility of so doing. Some assert that the teaching of spiritual values is the exclusive right and duty of the church and the home; others count that the proper exercise and very being of spiritual values is so enmeshed in religion that only an explicitly religious school can adequately teach them. These objectors claim that, on either basis, so long as the public school consistently maintains the historic American doctrine of the separation of church and state, so long must it remain inadequate to a proper teaching of the spiritual values necessary to our civilization.

Any such denial to the public school of either the right or the possibility of teaching the needed spiritual values we reject. Instead we propose to maintain both the logical possibility and the practical potential adequacy of the public school to teach such spiritual values as those named above and this on the basis of human reason and experience and without necessary recourse to religious authority. We propose further not only to uphold—under existing conditions of religious thought—the historic separation of church and state, but also to defend the moral and legal right of the public school to maintain and observe this separation consistently. It is the American way and we believe in it.

It may be well to emphasize the word *potential* in the phrase "potential practical adequacy." We do not claim that the current teaching practice in the public school is adequate to the developing of the spiritual quality needed in these spiritual values. We think, on the contrary, that the school tradition has in it too much of assigned tasks, rote memory, authoritarian control, and lack of actual social contact to develop the needed spiritual quality. The verb *to teach* itself needs to take on a more spiritual quality before it can fulfill its duty here. To help in these matters is a definite part of our program.

It may better define the problem and task of the book if we look closer into the character of our troubled times and see how out of them has come, on the one hand, a greater need for cultivating the spiritual values and, on the other, this hurtful distrust of our historic school procedure.

Even before World War II had come among us to threaten our civilization, things were not right in the world. A mistaken economic theory had tended to make men callously selfish. A misleading ethical theory had further encouraged the same selfishness. Meanwhile, the rate of modern discovery and invention had become so rapid that the social problems resulting from these changes had increased beyond our immediate ability to solve them. Each such unsolved social problem entails its social strain; and in many countries this mounting strain proved too great for the social structure to withstand. This, we may well believe, led many troubled souls to give up faith in themselves and seek instead some external authority upon which they might lean for guidance and support. Hogben in a striking phrase referred to this tendency as a "retreat from reason."[1] It seems highly probable that this tendency, working in countries where democracy had not been deeply grounded, helped to bring on fascism in its various forms and so helped to bring on the war. If the nineteenth century showed overconfidence in the easy effecting of human progress, this "retreat" marks a contrary reaction, specifically a widespread lessening of faith in man and in the processes

[1] Lancelot Hogben, *A Retreat from Reason* (New York: Random House, 1937).

In this little book Hogben makes clear that he is striking at a real phenomenon, a significant element in our current scene. But because the term "reason" was earlier used to imply primarily a reliance upon *a priori* reasoning from assumedly self-evident principles, the phrase is now open to possible misinterpretation. It is the use of intelligence in the inductive study of affairs that we herein wish especially to uphold.

of man's thought and discussion to deal with the practical affairs of life.

As this loss of faith became apparent, various groups sought to exploit it to their several ends. Certain social-political groups used it to make preparation for a day of desired violent revolution. To their program flocked many, especially the unemployed young people, both of our own country and elsewhere. As suggested, Mussolini and Hitler profited from this general breakdown of faith in ordinary human intelligence to build up their cult of dictatorship. Still other groups, religious in outlook, welcomed the loss of faith in man and sought to increase it by stressing anew such older doctrines as the inherent weakness and sinfulness of man, the hopelessness of any gospel of social improvement, and the inherent impotence of human reason against an element of irrationality said by them to be inherent in the nature of the universe. Thus, in part, it appears, arose Barthianism in Germany and neo-orthodoxy elsewhere.

Many who have accepted this "retreat from reason" as a movement to foster have especially attacked any consistently democratic education. Democratic teaching processes have been decried as soft and weakening, and a return has been advocated to older practices of "discipline" and indoctrination. It would not be true to say that all who have lost faith in man have cultivated their loss selfishly; the contrary in fact is true for many. But some long troubled at the unpopularity of certain of their doctrines have hailed this period of confusion and doubt as a long-sought opportunity and have endeavored to exploit it for the re-establishment of those losing doctrines. It is these last-named groups, it appears, who have been most active in spreading the doubt that the public school as thus far conducted is adequate to its spiritual task. And these have seized on the exclusion of religion from the public school as the particular point of alleged weakness, asserting that as long as this exclusion holds, the sole and necessary basis is lacking for the teaching of the spiritual values necessary for a proper civilization.

In our defense of the public school we wish it clearly understood that we intend no attack on religion. We do, however, assert our strong belief that all the youth of all the people should be educated together in the common public school and that the combined concern of all the people should foster and support this common school. We admit the legal right of any local group to organize a private school of its own; and it is possible that, under exceptional conditions, such a step might be wise and proper, especially where the aim is to initiate some worthy educational experiment or even perhaps to stage a needed public protest. But even so we wish to point to the attendant and inherent threat to the democratic process if such non-public schools should become so numerous or so permanent as to constitute an institutionalized rival to the common public school. The divisive effect of such rival systems within the body politic we believe to be hurtful, and this we hold whatever be the faith or cult or economic status or other divisive motive which supports the separation.

To clear up initial uncertainties, it may be well to give explicit consideration to the meanings herein to be given the key terms *civilization, spiritual values, public school,* and *separation of church and state.*

The term *civilization* is used, we find, in two senses that here concern us. In the one sense it is, as earlier suggested, the correlative of any culture. Each group, whether ancient Hittite or modern Swiss, lives its own culture, and the result is its civilization. In the other sense, the term is reserved for those groups whose cultural attainments if not admittedly higher in the scale are at any rate preferred to others. Many anthropologists question whether it is scientifically possible to prove the differences of value involved in assumed differences of level. We do not here enter upon an argument on the point, but say that when we of this book speak of the spiritual values necessary to an acceptable civilization we are following the second sense at least in preferring certain civilizations to others. And, it may be added, we shall later count it necessary to show how the necessary spiritual values are essential to the more desirable civilization.

The term *spiritual values* was implicitly defined earlier in this chapter where certain of these values were named as necessary to any satisfactory civilization. The same values have through the years been frequently discussed under the inclusive heading of "the true, the beautiful, and the good."

It is possible here to define the conception of spiritual values from an experiential point of view. To begin at the bottom, in all animal life there arise *wants*, hunger for example; and corresponding to any such want something may be found to satisfy it, as food satisfies hunger. Anything so answering a want we may call a *good*. This level of choosing, if we may so use the term, is shared by man with the brutes. We may accordingly call this the first or lowest level of evaluation.

But man goes higher. He finds that wants may thwart each other and that it pays—in the quality of life lived—to think before acting, to stop and think to choose in order to make life as good as possible, or more surely good, or at least to bring the fewest regrets. So to weigh goods against each other before choosing is to *evaluate* in the proper sense of the term. Man alone is capable of this valuing effort. To live a life characterized by such thoughtful choosing is to live on what we may call a higher or second level of evaluation.

But man can go still higher. Since the time of the Greeks, men have engaged in critical thinking. We can study critically the life process, how it proceeds, and what constitutes the good life seen at its best. For this we must study critically the terms we use in thinking and the principles involved in judging all the various parts and aspects of experience—right and wrong, truth, beauty. The values which emerge from such critical study constitute what we may call the third level of evaluation, the level of spiritual values in the full and proper sense. And we can say further of any step taken to move toward a higher level of thought and act, even from the lowest, that in so far as one moves consciously upward (as upward is here defined), doing this on the basis of consideration for fuller fitness, in that degree does he manifest true spiritual quality. We shall later return to a further elaboration of the definition of spiritual values—the whole book is in a sense such an exposition—but this preliminary discussion will, it is hoped, at least indicate the sense in which we are using the term *spiritual values*.

If anyone should object that we have in our usage deflected the term *spiritual* from what he calls its true and necessary meaning, in that our usage carries no explicit or necessary reference to religious or divine authority or sanction, our reply would be that recognized usage gives no such necessary reference. On the contrary, there are various recognized meanings, among them one which to be sure does carry this religious implication; but there are other meanings which amply support the usage we have adopted. Some might prefer another term than spiritual values for expressing what we here have in mind, possibly higher values or, simply, values. We grant to these, of course, full right to their judgment, but we think the term spiritual more adequately implies the richer content we are thinking of than does any alternative. In fact, we feel that if our book can help spread this usage of the term spiritual, it will be better all round; specifically, that it may make for better agreement among diverse groups. It may be added finally that we mean in adopting the term no commitment to any dualism but rather the contrary; and just as truly we mean no asceticism. As we thus uphold the spiritual values in experience, it is the good life we seek, the life good to live; and we seek it for all and as far as is humanly possible to effect it on terms of equality for all.

The term *public school* as here used is of course easily defined. By it we mean specifically the American type of public school—publicly controlled and publicly supported—and, especially for present purposes, one run consistently on the American doctrine of the separation of church and state.

The term *separation of church and state* is likewise easily defined for the purposes here under consideration. We understand by this term the doctrine that the state shall not appropriate money to religious institutions and shall not prefer one religious outlook as such to another; and that the state will protect its citizens in the equal free exercise of thought and choice in matters religious and will require of its schools that they not teach or act in any way to contravene these principles.

In the matter of teaching, we believe specifically that there is a large area of ground common for both public school teachers and religious teachers to the end that they should have common concern for the spiritual values herein upheld and can likewise find a common support for those values. Outside of this common ground, into the area of religious authority, the public school teacher as such may not go, while therein the religious teacher is free to teach as to him seems right. We then, explicitly, affirm the full right of any religious group to add, under its separate teaching auspices, any religious authority or any non-socially-hurtful religious considerations it may choose. But we do pointedly reject and oppose any denial by such religious groups of the full right of the public school to teach the named spiritual values and their like on any grounds of validity which human reason can with due critical care choose to defend.

Chapter II

COMMUNITY AND SPIRITUAL VALUES

I T IS perhaps too easy to think of spiritual values in an
abstract fashion. Long historical association of the spiritual
with the immaterial no doubt has taught us to do this. To con-
sign spiritual values exclusively to the realm of the immaterial
would be a misfortune, however. For spiritual values to be
effective in conduct, it is tremendously important to study
them in their material matrix of practical everyday social and
individual endeavor.

There are various reasons why this matrix is important. In
the first place, the teaching of spiritual values under public
auspices requires an examination of the limits within which
there is a public community of spiritual values. In the second
place, the particular structure of a community and the manner
in which it functions cannot help but largely condition the
kind of spiritual values which are to be perpetuated through
the school. In the third place, the sense of community itself
carries a considerable cargo of spiritual value. In the fourth
place, it is only through a social matrix, of which the public
school is but a single instance, that any values can be taught and
learned. Each of these points needs now to be elaborated in
some detail.

THE COMMUNAL ACCEPTANCE OF SPIRITUAL VALUES

It is the contention of this Yearbook that the limits within
which spiritual values can and are being taught in the public
school are much broader than is ordinarily recognized. The
first step in the expansion of this thesis is to note that the ordi-

nary limits within which anything can be taught in the public school are those which define areas of common agreement in the community whose school it is. In fact, herein lies the very genesis of the public school itself. Its conception and birth definitely had to wait till a community of opinion favorable to its existence could be brought about.

Conversely it can be said that the public character of the school is limited by the extent to which it has community backing. Thus even at its birth it was noted that the public school carried a birthmark: Controversial subjects like religion and slavery were excluded from its curriculum because no community of opinion had developed in these areas as yet. In other words, the limits of the curriculum of the public school involve a study of community as much as, if not more than, a study of educational policy.

Before proceeding to discover whether there is a sufficient community of opinion about spiritual values to include them in the public school curriculum, it may be well to say a word more about the nature of community. Every individual has had some experience as a member of a social group. He has probably been a member of a number of different groups at the same time. Into some of these groups he has been born a member, as, for instance, in the case of the family and the state. Into others he has entered voluntarily, as in the case of many churches. But in all these cases the distinctive feature that makes individuals into a social group is some common purpose or purposes which they are pursuing together. If there were no such common purpose, the individuals would be just an agglomeration. Between an agglomeration and a well-knit social group there are, of course, many degrees. Between these two extremes the measure of socialization will be proportioned by the extent to which there is a community of interest among those involved.

It is well to bear in mind this matter of degree of community in endeavoring to determine whether the community is sufficiently agreed on spiritual values to include them in the program of the public school. In so complex a matter it is possible that the community is agreed on some aspects of the teaching of spiritual values but disagreed on others. Indeed the Yearbook would like to make exactly that point. It holds that there is a large measure of agreement in American communities on what these spiritual values mean by way of actual personal conduct. Our differences, our lack of community, on them concerns rather the philosophical rationalization and verbalizing of these values.

To employ but one example, there is a united community demand that children learn to be just in their dealings with each other. The demand for fair play extends all the way from the sports program to learning to take turns in the kindergarten. Indeed, children are more likely to overlook creed and color in their schoolmates than are their elders in their associates. But when it comes to teaching the why and wherefore of just conduct, there is a plethora, almost a confusion, of advice. Some find justification in the natural rights of man, some in the grounds of expediency, some in tested consequences, and some in the ordinance of God.

Unhappily in the history of education the school has been more concerned with the verbalization of justice—and the rest of the array of spiritual values—than it has with just conduct. It is easy to see how this came about. For the most part, except in the case of primitive societies, teachers have taught school, not life. Or, if they have taught life, it has been about life rather than life itself. The easiest way to teach about life is through symbols. Of course, the chief symbols have been words, especially words representing ideas. In the course of time teachers became so preoccupied with ideas that ideas came to outrank the action for which they stood. Yet it is in the sphere of ideas that the contrary winds of opinion blow. Because these winds strained the solidarity of community, the nineteenth century developed the tradition that the public school should not be concerned with controversial issues. Besides, in the nineteenth century teaching techniques had not yet developed to a point where controversial issues could be managed. Teaching at that time still meant to inculcate or indoctrinate a single point of view. Curriculum content which could not by common consent be conformed to this method necessarily had to be left out. Unfortunately many lay and professional people interpreted this tradition as casting out or at least disregarding problems of daily conduct as well as problems involving philosophical subtleties.

As a matter of fact, at the level of conduct it has proved impossible to throw spiritual values out of the public school curriculum. The teacher might slight or disregard them but exclude them he could not. Return to the case of justice just mentioned. It almost defies imagination how a public school could be carried on from day to day without pupil relations posing such conflicts of interest as demand just settlement. However the settlement is made, the whole experience will inescapably result in the children learning something about justice in the concrete as well as possibly in the abstract.

Now, from the point of view of community, which is more important—that justice be done and habits of justice be formed in the child or that the child have correct verbalizations, correct "ideas," about justice? If community had to wait on its members' seeing eye to eye or on a meeting of their minds, it is doubtful whether communities as large as those supporting public schools would ever be formed. The fact is that community can and does exist where individuals agree on just the form of overt conduct. To be sure, the community will be all the stronger if agreement on conduct can be reinforced by similarity of idea or philosophy about conduct as well. But community, especially democratic community because of its high regard for individual differences, must be pragmatic; it must at any given moment be content with community at whatever level of unity of the one and the many it can achieve.

Indeed, once a measure of it has been secured, should that measure be thrown out or disregarded merely because the whole cannot be achieved? The answer is clearly no. The conclusion therefore seems to follow that the public school can and should aim much more intensively than it has at the inculcation of habits embodying spiritual values. Certainly this is preferable to having the public school curriculum draw a complete blank in spiritual values merely because it is now and perhaps always will be impossible to achieve a united community on the philosophy supporting them.

To some this result may seem to be placing the value of community ahead of that of principle. But this is really not so. It is merely recognizing that there are degrees of community. A most notable instance of the balance between the unity of community and the diversity of principle is to be found in our national democracy. There we have overwhelming community on such spiritual values as respect for personality, freedom of conscience, thought, and speech. But we have been so greatly at odds in stating the ultimate grounds for our faith in these values that the American community has had to resolve itself into subdivisions to suit the various individuals concerned. The basic subdivision here is that between church and state. Yet it needs pointing out that in spite of the incompatibility of viewpoint which has forced the divorce of church and state, there is nonetheless a large degree of national unity in this country. It is this national unity on the spiritual values of our democracy and civilization which should inspire confidence that the limits of our American community are wide enough to have such values included in the public school curriculum.

Even in the controversial area of philosophical theory there is more common ground for the teaching of spiritual values in the public school than is ordinarily recognized. In point of educational philosophy the major difficulty centers on the adjective "spiritual." Both historically and in the popular mind "spiritual" is not only associated with the immaterial but frequently with the supernatural as well. The supernatural is a bone of contention both among those who disagree on the attributes of the supernatural and among those who deny the supernatural altogether. The latter are inclined to take a naturalistic view of spiritual values. Of course the supernatural-ists are opposed to such naturalism. But what is often over-looked is the fact that the supernaturalists recognize a natural order as well as a supernatural one. Their objection to the naturalists is not that they assert an order of nature but that they assert the order of nature is the only order and that there is no other. Now, whether or not there is a supernatural order beyond the natural, it does seem as if the naturalists and super-naturalists should be able to find some community of interest at least in the order of nature which they both recognize.

Such a community of interest might take two directions. On the one hand it might be based on the fact that spiritual values are not exclusively supernatural. Perhaps, as already suggested, they are in part what have been called "higher" or more enduring values. Their claim to this quality would be based on their history in the natural order. The virtues (habits) embodying such spiritual values may be called natural virtues. On the other hand agreement between the naturalists and the supernaturalists can readily be found in the fact that spiritual values, however conceived, must be realized in the natural order. What they demand of children and adults in the natural course of conduct admits of little or none of the disagreement raised by theoretical questions about their ultimate meaning or sanction. Here the distinction between natural and supernatural is akin to that already drawn between conduct and its rationalization.

Although restricting discourse on spiritual values to natural-ism may afford common ground for the inclusion of spiritual values in the public school curriculum, there are many super-naturalists who will think such a restriction too high a price to pay for community. If they persist in their loyalty to supernatural principles, there is imminent danger that the community will have to be subdivided so that spiritual values may be taught in various private and independent schools. But just before they do that, one further resource should be investigated. Historically the Christian church has claimed to be a wide community whose limits include all men of good will whether believers or pagans.[1] The public school has much in common with such a community for it is composed of children who come from many diverse faiths and whose youthful innocence is earnest of their good will. Surely such an approach to community should afford a base for the public school's teaching of spiritual values, even if all other suggestions fail.

Every effort should be made to find some basis of community. The luxury of going our own separate ways in the teaching of spiritual values is too expensive. The danger which threatens, if we fail to establish a community of interest in the spiritual values of our civilization, has been amply and conclusively demonstrated by the events leading up to the Second World War. Not only did we lack thoroughgoing confidence in the spiritual values of our democracy but we were divided in our support of the ones we did accept. In the face of a hard-hitting, subtle, and wily enemy we had difficulty in presenting a united front in defense of our values. This must not happen again. It need not happen again if we will sincerely and persistently pursue the basis of community which will recognize the teaching of spiritual values in the public school.

SPIRITUAL VALUES CONDITIONED BY COMMUNITY

In seeking to establish a community with broad enough limits to permit the inclusion of spiritual values in the public school curriculum it is also necessary to be sure that we mean the same things by the spiritual values selected. The inquiry

---

[1] Protestants refer to this community as the "holy catholic church" or the "church universal," while Catholics call it the "mystical body of Christ."

into whether we mean the same things should be pursued in two directions. In the first place it is now time to indicate in some detail, though by no means exhaustively, what is the sort of spiritual values of civilization which this Yearbook affirms can and should be taught in the public school. In the second place it will be well to inquire how these values and their teaching are affected by conditioning sociological factors, such as whether the community be democratic or fascistic, individualistic or collectivistic, and the like.

Community Functions as Spiritual Values. The spiritual values of civilized community life tend on the whole to be closely patterned after the structure of community and the way it functions. We saw earlier that community is composed of individuals who find themselves gathered together in a number of different clusters for the pursuit of common ends or interests. We note further the bi-polar quality of community. One pole is the individual and the other society—that is, other individuals. The single individual is born into society, and a need for society, other individuals, is born into him. Moreover, the single individual is born with potential capacities which crave expression. He needs others, however, to show him the ways in which he will be able to exercise his capacities to an optimum. These others he may need directly in face-to-face relations or he may profit from them vicariously through written accounts of their experience or through artifacts which they make available. Indeed, without this funded capital of others' experience, the social heritage, the potential capacities of the single individual, would be severely stunted in its growth.

Similarly, the cohesiveness of society depends in large measure on the ways in which different individuals complement each other. The sharing of common ends or interests depends in the first instance on having some common end to pursue. But it depends in the second place on the unique contribution which each individual can make toward that common end.

Thus in pursuit of the common end each becomes dependent upon the other for the unique ingredient which he indispensably contributes to the final goal. The advantage of dependency is that it permits specialization. Instead of the individual's trying independently and laboriously to make up for his own inadequacies, involvement in society permits him to specialize and intensify along the lines of his special gifts and aptitudes. From either view it is this mutual dependency, it is the way in which individuals complement each others' efforts, which makes mightily for cohesiveness in society.

The foregoing is not simply descriptive of the structure and function of community. It is also normative; implicit in it is a scheme of values. These considerations point to a pattern, an ideal, of what the individual "ought" to do. In order for the individual to derive the benefits of community, there are certain spiritual values which he must adopt and pursue.

Co-operation is obviously one of the chief of these. Co-operation is activity based on conscious awareness by the individual of his dependence on others or a conscious awareness of the way in which individuals complement each other. When he designedly promotes this mutuality, he is pursuing a spiritual value. Inherent in this value is a nest of other spiritual values. These are more easily described when it is realized that there are frequently obstacles in the way of the ready achievement of co-operation. To be sure, individuality best realizes itself in co-operation with other individualities. But at the same time it is often self-assertive. Instead of complementing other individualities, it often finds itself in conflict with them. What it wishes for the realization of its own potentialities is also desired by someone else. Where the supply of this commodity is limited, the spiritual value or virtue of co-operation is thus put under severe strain. If at this point either or both individuals can learn to restrain their self-assertiveness, it is found that other spiritual values are generated.

Self-denial or temperance is one of these. Obviously, if one can restrain himself in such a situation, a clash of interest is avoided and co-operation can go forward. This is a difficult value or virtue to achieve; yet civilized communities have been so dependent upon it for their continued existence that it is small wonder it ranks high in the roster of spiritual values. It is also deeply involved in the persistence and tenacity so necessary to achieving good things that are difficult to do. Self-denial is not only a part of moral fiber but it ranks so high with some that they make an absolute of it. They encourage individuals to adopt the ascetic life, the life of self-discipline, as an end in itself.

Self-denial reaches its highest spiritual quality in the act of self-sacrifice. This act is usually only called for on such stern occasions as when the community is in serious physical danger. In self-sacrifice the individual gives striking recognition to the tremendous spiritual value of community, to the fact that if there is no community, according to his convictions, his worth as an individual is of little account.

In self-sacrifice other spiritual values are shown, such as bravery and courage. For individuals who are naturally self-assertive, to run the risk of self-extinction takes high qualities of heart and mind. Again, these spiritual values are not just limited to risks of physical danger. To defend an unpopular point of view, to risk fame and reputation in a cause of conscience, to break the crust of custom by pioneering a startling innovation are also instances requiring great fortitude.

There are positive spiritual values which promote co-operation and community as well as the ones of negation and denial just considered. Notable among these is kindness. Kindness is an important lubricant of social contact. It prevents friction when the irregularities of individuality rub against each other. Perhaps it is even more important in the effect it has on the undeveloped potentialities of individual capacity. It tends to draw it out, to encourage it to activate itself. Unlike cruelty or malice, kindness provides the friendly warmth so necessary for all growing things. In intensified form it becomes the spiritual value of charity and love.

The positive attitudes of kindness and love are more readily entered upon where individuals have an understanding of each other. To be able to get the other fellow's point of view, especially in what he suffers, is an act of great spiritual value. Through sympathy one understands the shortcomings of others which impede community action. Through tact he is able to act so as not to aggravate these inadequacies but rather to overcome them. Sympathy and tact thus not only afford spiritual value but also provide a subtle means of communication solidifying community.

Another spiritual value more positive in its promotion of co-operation is that of generosity. If community depends on sharing of common purpose, then generosity is an intensification of sharing. It extends, not to just the common purpose, but to all the resources great and small that are involved in achieving it. Whenever there is a limited supply of either the material or the immaterial culture, the sharing of one's store of it with another is a social act of great importance. And to share with another beyond what the bare necessities of the case demand is especially deserving in spiritual value.

In spite of the wide common acceptance of the spiritual values examined so far, they do not seem actually to enter so simply into the motives of men. The virtues or habits based upon them are difficult to form. Perhaps this is because, as already mentioned, they tend to run counter to the individual's natural self-assertiveness. In any case, this situation leads to the mention of another spiritual value which is employed to reinforce all the preceding ones. It is sense of duty. Most of us will acknowledge that it is good to do what he ought to do, that there are other interests than merely those of self-assertion. Sense of duty reminds the individual that if he wants to participate in the values of community, he must not do things destructive of community. In a community, the enjoyment of the benefits of a right on the part of one individual usually implies the imposition of the burden of a duty on some other individual. Hence individuals must be equally ready to under-take duties as well as to exercise rights. Obviously a community cannot long endure where individuals are concerned only with their rights and forget their sense of duty.

Another spiritual value which performs a community func-tion similar to sense of duty is loyalty. Loyalty is what keeps the individual performing his duties even when those about him are failing in theirs. He sticks by his associates through thick and thin. The spiritual value of loyalty seems to rise in proportion to the strength of forces which would rend the community asunder. Loyalty is a social matrix which binds individuals together, giving them the sense of being members one of another.

So much for the idealization into spiritual values of the things which the individual must do in order to promote the mutuality of community. In similar fashion the community's dependence on the individuality of its members is also idealized into a further set of spiritual values. While the community is expecting the individual to hold in check his native tendency to self-assertion, it must remember not to thwart this tendency completely, but only to co-ordinate it with a similar tendency in others. Indeed, it is only through preserving as much leeway as possible for self-assertion that each will grow in control of his own destiny. There is a uniqueness about each individual which must be preserved; his personality must be respected. One of the greatest spiritual values of our civilization has been summarized in the imperative to treat the individual always as an end and never as a means merely.

To have a high regard for the spiritual worth of the in-dividual requires a community to regard him not so much for what he now is as for what he can do, what he can potentially achieve. Circumstances of birth, in other words, should not be the measure of his opportunities. Race, color, economic status of parents, and the like are accidents; they are irrelevant as an index of potential capacity. In the degree that a community makes provision for each person to have an opportunity to do that thing for which he is most fitted, it is, as Plato said, a just society. Obviously, then, justice is yet another of the spiritual values a community must seek for its members.

Regard for individuality is further to be found in the spiritual values associated with freedom. Individuality cannot assert itself unless it is in some measure free and unhampered to do so. This is why civil, religious, and academic freedoms are rated among the most cherished of all spiritual values to which man has aspired. The community will do well to remember not only that these liberties are the indispensable atmosphere in which individuality sustains itself but that the variations they permit are also indispensable as the device by which community progressively redirects itself to richer and fuller living. The community will also do well to remember that freedom can only breathe in an atmosphere of tolerance. Tolerance, like self-denial, yields its own peculiar spiritual value.

Granted respect for individuality and freedom to exercise their potential capacities, the simple fulfillment of these capacities brings a train of other spiritual values. One of the simplest forms of self-fulfillment is play. The exercise of one's capacities just because they were designed by nature for exercise, or, as we say, just for the fun of exercising them, is one of the earliest joys of childhood. It is to the lasting credit of Froebel that he taught educators to see the educational and spiritual value of play. The community without games and festivals, therefore, is to that degree impoverished in spiritual value.

Perhaps in this connection one thinks next of the spiritual values which emerge from the practice of the arts, especially, though by no means exclusively, of the fine arts. Sensitivity to, if not creative manipulation of, color, line, and sound is accompanied by joys that are their own reward. They give a sense of self-fulfillment not to be missed in any community.

But, as already hinted, this sense of self-fulfillment can be gained in the agricultural and industrial arts as well as in the pursuit of the fine arts. Work as well as leisure has its spiritual fruits. The community which would fail to idealize the satisfaction which flows from work well done would be deficient in a most precious spiritual value. Moreover, the management of daily affairs requires a combination of moral and intellectual virtues whose balanced exercise produces the spiritual value of prudence.

Not to be overlooked in the spiritual values of self-fulfillment are those which have to do with the exercise of the higher reflective processes. One need not necessarily agree with Aristotle's conclusion, that the highest end of thought is to contemplate thought, in order to participate in the delights of mental effort. These are of the highest excellence whether the individual is engaged in philosophical speculation or in scientific experimentation. The achievement of logical and systematic thought provides a sense of spiritual satisfaction well authenticated by many centuries of civilization.

Variation of Spiritual Values According to the Form of Community. So far, spiritual values have been stated in terms of community in the hope that a maximum of agreement might be elicited for the feasibility of teaching these values in the public schools. But it would be a mistake not to realize that so far community has been described only in the most general terms; that the spiritual values examined have been, after all, the spiritual values of almost any community. Thus the sacrifice, sense of duty, loyalty, and the like could be taught in the public schools of fascism as well as those of democracy. This even holds true in some measure for such spiritual values as kindness, generosity, and to a limited extent for justice and freedom.

The fact that these latter values have only a limited application to a fascist community points to the need for a brief discussion of the effect on spiritual values that differing kinds of community organization have. For instance, democracy and fascism differ on whether the community itself has any spiritual values peculiarly its own to fulfill. Where no distinction is made between the community and the state, as in the case of fascism, it is generally thought that the social group in its entirety, in its totality (hence totalitarianism), has values which absorb or transcend those of its members. This must necessarily be so for those holding this view because the state is the link between generations and is therefore presumably more farseeing and less selfish. This being the case, some of the spiritual values already mentioned would have to be devalued, especially those exalting individuality.

In democracy, however, the state is only one among a number of different social groups into which the community is organized and subdivided. In such a setup, community organization is a means, not an end. Hence spiritual fulfillment is that of its members. Therefore, it is more than probable that in a democratic community the foregoing spiritual values, particularly those emphasizing respect for individuality, justice, and liberty, would be enhanced rather than diminished.

What is true of differences in the political organization of the community is equally true of its economic organization. The spiritual values to be gained from satisfaction in work well done have been mentioned. To gain this sense of self-fulfillment, however, the concurrent circumstances of employment must be conducive to this end. Periodic unemployment, excessively long hours of work, inadequate pay, and inadequate insurance against the risks of health and old age are emphatically not the conditions of any proper sense of self-fulfillment.

For many people the spiritual values examined here will thrive best in an atmosphere of relative economic security. In other words, the individual must be assured the opportunity to do useful and creative work at a rate of pay which, with thrifty management, is able to command both the necessities and the amenities of life. Among the necessities prerequisite to the realizing of spiritual values are adequate food, shelter, and clothing together with insurance against dependency in sickness and old age. Among the amenities to be mentioned especially as conducive to the generation and enjoyment of spiritual values are opportunities for recreation and avocation.

As much as economic security supports spiritual values, a community must be constantly on its guard that security does not lull individuals into sluggish inertia. Self-fulfillment is only possible through self-activity. Hence, the security mentioned here is intended not to enervate but to energize the pursuit of spiritual values. A further characteristic of the economic order, then, consistent with this view is that it provides for some freedom for individual enterprise. Negatively this means that the individual must be able to carry on his economic productivity free from irresponsible private power and unregulated monopolies on the one hand and from compulsory labor and arbitrary public authority on the other. Affirmatively it means adventure in employing ingenuity to adapt means to ends in developing both materials and methods for satisfying economic wants.

Obviously the foregoing economic conditions cannot be realized without some restraint on individual economic interests. This is particularly true in the area of acquisition and management of private property. The adjudication of conflicting interests here will place a great strain on people's sense of justice. To insure the spiritual values of justice there must be not only equality before the law but equal access to justice in fact. This equal access must be open to all regardless of the way present inequalities of wealth may permit the well-to-do to exhaust more remedies of the law than the poor can afford.

THE SPIRITUAL VALUE OF COMMUNITY

The sense of community may itself be a spiritual value which the public school might well seek out. Making common cause with others has given comfort, assurance, and inspiration in many different kinds of enterprise. The spiritual values which flow from a sense of belonging have been authenticated for centuries. The early Christians drew no less strength from their congregations than do moderns as they organize their nations for war. Furthermore, the spiritual value inherent in a sense of community is found in defeat as well as in victory.

From this point of view the public school can tap latent spiritual resources. Instead of being devoid of spirituality there is perhaps no type of school which has so much to offer. Public schools gather together children of a diversity of race, religion, economic status, and national origin. Few other agencies have such a unique opportunity to develop cohesiveness predicated on interdependence. What a temple the public school offers for encouraging and celebrating both the spiritual values cherishing individuality and those fostering mutuality!

COMMUNITY AND THE COMMUNICATION OF SPIRITUAL VALUES

Deriving spiritual value from a sense of belonging to a community has educational as well as spiritual significance. The community is not only a source of spiritual inspiration but the key to educational method as well. Although the detailed significance of this statement will be developed in later chapters, a few main principles may be outlined here.

It has already been asserted as the esesntial nature of community that individuals are gathered together in the pursuit of common ends. To pursue common ends implies that the individuals concerned to some degree think alike about their ends. This suggests that common ends or community depend in some measure on communication between individuals. Indeed, we have substantiation for this position in that oft-quoted remark of Dewey's that "Society not only continues to exist *by* transmission, *by* communication, but it may fairly be said to exist *in* transmission, *in* communication."[2]

[2] John Dewey, *Democracy and Education*, New York, Macmillan Co., 1916, p. 5.

But, as already indicated, communication is more than a mere matter of exchange of verbal symbols. It involves conduct as well. A symbol must mean the same kind of conduct to all who employ it. Stated conversely, all must participate in the conduct it denotes with the same meanings. In fact, here is the great educational significance of community. One learns to communicate with others—that is, one becomes a member of a community—by participating in its activities. Indeed, it is only through participation that one can be sure that he is communicating, that is, getting the same meanings out of the same symbols.

So we re-emphasize the happy coincidence that there is spiritual value in community and that participation in community is the chief avenue to a learning, understanding, and possession of spiritual values. These conclusions perhaps give further meaning to the fact that spiritual values are themselves usually the idealization of the way community structure functions. All this points to the grave importance of defining the limits of community widely enough to include the teaching of spiritual values in the public school.

Chapter III

THE ORIGIN, DEVELOPMENT, AND VALIDITY OF SPIRITUAL VALUES

SPIRITUAL VALUES FURTHER DEFINED

IN CHAPTER I we gave a preliminary definition of spiritual values. Now we wish to carry the analysis further, first by asking about the term *value* and then by suggesting how we shall use the term *spiritual values*.

It appears desirable to conceive our guiding ideas in terms of life processes. For such conceptions, we believe, are more defensible in experience and therefore better suited to public school treatment. The life process in man, as in the other animals, manifests itself in responses to situations—to situations that emerge to and for the organism as it and the environment interact. Any such human response will, if definite enough, manifest itself internally as a felt *want*, hunger for example, and externally as movements or efforts to meet the want. In such a case whatever is found to satisfy the want, as food satisfies hunger or drink satisfies thirst, we call a *good*. Clearly so complex an organism as man may be expected to have more wants than would a simpler organization and, consequently, to require a greater variety of goods.

It may well happen that two simultaneous wants conflict so that both cannot be attained. I may, for instance, want (wish) to sleep longer than 7:30 A.M., but I also want (desire) to meet my 9 o'clock engagement. In such case I have to choose; I cannot do both. In this way it often becomes necessary to judge among wants (or their goods) so as to decide which to choose in order to make the resulting life effects best, or more surely good, or at least to bring fewest regrets. And in such judging one weighs in terms of what one counts as prospective good, the desirable life to seek, all things considered. What behavior properly to count the good life is a question we postpone for the present, but every judging assumes some conception of the good and each successive judging, itself being judged by its outcomes, helps to build one's guiding conception.

To judge critically among competing wants or goods is to *evaluate*, and the respective worths so adjudged we call comparative values. The term *value* thus implies a good which has passed through the process of examination and evaluation. From such a process a value gets attached to it certain conditions and implications which facilitate judging and choice, immediately for the case in hand but as a rule serviceable also later. To sleep after 7:30 may be permissible where no conflict is involved; it may be necessary when I am ill. To refuse to sleep late will be necessary—and so morally obligatory—if I have a 9 o'clock engagement with no contrary reason, like illness, sufficient to break it. It is in this way that the process of evaluating attaches to the emerging value its quota of qualifying conditions and implications.

As we watch men face life's varied situations which call thus for weighing, we find great diversity of attitude and practice. And we who thus observe tend to judge men by the way they judge situations. Some we find living much like animals, acting simply on the impulse of the moment or at best following blind custom. These we place on a low level of esteem; we think they should do better. And doing better means for most of us, and especially for the more thoughtful among us, more or less of such things as (1) being sensitive in the general area so as more surely to catch up any case properly demanding consideration; (2) considering not simply how I feel now, my present impulse, but taking into account how I shall later feel and think as I look back more broadly on the matter, so to act now as to avoid later regrets; and (3) weighing not simply to consider my own wishes, as do thoughtless and selfish men, but to give due weight to others involved, for their rights and feelings as individuals or perhaps for the common good of us all. What constitutes "due weight" is not easy to state in advance; it will vary from situation to situation. But one principle most of us use in judging, at least in our best moods, is to give no greater weight to one's own desires than to those of others similarly involved. The Golden Rule, in short, is a useful principle in judging situations where moral values are at stake.

In all of this, it may be added that to give highest quality to present conduct there must be conscious intent to do the right thing (whatever honest study may show that to be) coupled with conscious attention to what is being done, that its bearing on life may be best. And, still further, there must be present along with the intent to do the right thing a conscious sense of double responsibility for what one is doing, responsibility to respect others' rights involved and responsibility to one's self to live up to the best one can reasonably find. It is on the basis of behavior so managed in all these various respects that we judge the conduct and characters of men.

As we think ill of those who habitually disregard these various considerations, so we think highly of those who respect and obey them. We may then say that in the degree that one does in his heart and life give true respect to the varied considerations set out in the two preceding paragraphs, in like degree do his life and conduct show spiritual quality. And similarly, for one who consciously moves from a lesser to a greater inherent manifestation of such conduct, we say that he too is thus far showing spiritual quality.

A value, we saw, is a good that has gone through the process of conscious test. After evaluation we know somewhat of when and how and where that good is to be chosen, somewhat of when it is in general less desirable or more desirable to be used. Some values will rank higher than others either in the frequency of their general availability for use or in their strategic value for good when used, and some will rank high in both respects. We may thus think informally of a scale of values ranged according to their probable serviceability for good. Those that rank high on such a scale we call the spiritual values.

The foregoing definition of spiritual quality and values came by way of evaluation in the moral realm, an area which for many yields the clearest and surest examples. But there are other areas in which, by common consent, spiritual quality is likewise present and in consequence of which other spiritual values are similarly to be found. The reference is specifically to intellectual and to aesthetic goods. These two areas, with that of the moral or ethical, make the trio—the true, the beautiful, and the good—of classical philosophy.

In these two areas, as was found above in the moral, there may be goods where value (as previously defined) is not properly to be ascribed. The animal mother may show what is to us humans a high regard for the welfare of her young; but this quality thus pleasing to us is not, we must believe, similarly pleasing to her mate or her fellows. They make no conscious evaluation of what she does or does not do as to the service it performs for the young. Similarly for aesthetic appreciation, the peacock attracts his female by a gorgeous array of color and the flower similarly attracts the bee and the butterfly; but we cannot allow conscious evaluation of what thus attracts. And the same lack of value as such may hold for humans with respect to certain of their intellectual and aesthetic goods. These goods must pass through the process of evaluation before they are on the way to acceptance as having spiritual quality.

When intellectual and aesthetic values have emerged through conscious appraisal and so carry with them recognized conditions and qualifications as to when and how to use them, how and why and wherein they may be serviceable, so that we may here also have the basis for scale-making, then we may ascribe spiritual quality to the elements on such a scale and spiritual value to those higher placed on the scale. In these spiritual values refinement holds sway—refinement of thought (logical quality) in the intellectual realm, refinement of perception and bearing in the aesthetic; and with it all an implication of tendency to raise the quality of the resulting human living. For the sake of a certain future application we may add here that those men who are sufficiently talented by nature and care enough to accumulate and organize many successive experiences of personal evaluation may therein build themselves into experts—scholars or artists as the case may be—capable in higher than usual degree in judging such matters.

Such values thus relate to consciously formed ideals or standards for judging conduct or procedure in any areas of life where ideals or standards have been carefully built. Men learn by experience that certain ways of thinking or feeling or acting are better than others, that some are more likely to bring considered satisfaction while others bring regret. Out of many such experiences through the ages of trying out various proposals men build ideals and standards by which to judge the good life both in its general character and in its necessary details. Spiritual quality, we may then say, inheres either in the conscious building of such ideals, whether in the individual or in the group, or in the conscious effort to realize them. Spiritual values on this basis are the higher range of the specific values sought in and through established ideals, judging higher those values which either promise more generally to serve for good or promise when used to bring greater good or promise better under both heads.

THE GROUP CULTURE

The history of man as man began, we are told, somewhere from one to five million years ago. Some time after that beginning there also began that long slow accumulation of human experience we call the culture. We can be reasonably sure that at first its growth, judged by the rate we now know, was very, very slow. Even after all of this beginning period except our last 50,000 years, man (*homo sapiens*) passed 25,000 years without improving upon his chipped flint axe and then another 10,000 years with this now ground and polished axe before he displaced it with a bronze one, and still again 1,000 years before he displaced this with an iron axe. The rate was improving, but it was still slow.

Slow, however, as the rate may seem, it leaves us the more certain that man himself made his own advances and that he made them as we now see him making the analogous advances, namely, by using his sensitivity, his insight, and his wit, especially in connection with what he had previously found out. It is this last-named factor of the accumulated culture, growing now much greater, which explains the recent more rapid rate of advance.

The question we are here to study is how man effected his spiritual culture, at least that part of it which specifically concerns the public school. As we study this culture we find three highly fruitful early advances: language, tools, and selfhood. The long achieving of these, it seems probable, went on simultaneously, each mutually helping to bring the other two into more effective existence. And this process of mutually interactive building went on, we may suppose, even for many thousand years; the process is in fact not yet finished—and never will be—for all three lines of advance can and will continue each to make additions to the other two.

As regards language, we can further distinguish three far-reaching bearings it has on life: one to aid communication, obvious from the first; a second to aid thinking, less obvious but no less true even from the beginning; the third to bring criticism, a higher level of thinking effective much later, in fact only within written history. That language aids communication was of course true as soon and as fast as language was achieved; and with it came more extensive and more effective co-operation. As to the improvement of thinking by language, we have to consider how human speech differs from animal cries. The crucial difference seems to be that the animal cry is his organic reaction to what disturbs him, and this disturbed response serves to stir his fellows, while human speaking (or gesturing) is a consciously chosen means for stirring the other person to think in a fore-intended way. Man in fact exhibits both human speech and animal excitation. When he blushes, this may tell a definite story; but the blushing was not a gesture chosen to carry the story. More likely, on the contrary, the blushing tells what one would prefer to hide. But speech (including gesture), in the degree that it is typically present, is essentially a thought-out, a consciously chosen, measure for making the other person think what one intends him to think. Such a process then is of necessity limited to a self-other type of organism (as we shall in a moment consider).

Accordingly, in the degree that speech is true speech, it is, as it were, tried out in advance upon one's self before it is turned loose to affect the other person. Careful language is then at bottom a thinking, a thinking before it is an utterance. Thinking thus is a man talking with himself.[1] The objective effect of language on its users is to improve both speech and thinking. Each of these two had to help bring the other into fuller existence, since neither is possible except in terms of the other, as both are possible only in a self-other type of selfhood.

The third result of language is criticism. To name a thought or a distinction is to give it objective existence, so that people can confer over it. This possibility, first realized in high degree among the Greeks, gives to thought a new dimension which carries it to levels inconceivable not only to the lower animals

---

[1] "If we had never talked with others and they with us, we should never talk to and with ourselves." John Dewey, *Experience and Nature*, Chicago and London, Open Court Publishing Co., 1925, p. 170.

but even to untutored man. Language and the self-other character of human personality have together given us the higher character of the human mind.

The achieving of this self-other compounded selfhood is so important that specific attention to it becomes necessary. For it is such a selfhood that constitutes the essence of man's power to conceive and live the spiritual values we are concerned in this book to support.

SELF-OTHER SELFHOOD

It is surprising how easily people take for granted the essential difference between man and the lower animals. Many if asked about it hasten to "explain" the difference by saying that man alone has an immortal soul and that it is this soul at work within man which gives him his distinctive human characteristics. And these same people often go on to ask how anyone who denies immortality can explain the obvious differences between man and the higher animals. But the more closely we study the problem, the more surely we seem to find that everything of distinctively human behavior is learned, and the less it appears probable that the fact of immortality can explain the difference between man and brute. In fact, the problem of explanation exists as truly for the affirmers of immortality as for its deniers, namely to explain helpfully how the human child born as ignorant as the lower animals, and often more helpless, grows psychologically into the selfhood we know.

The story of Kamala, the wolf-child of the Midnapore (India) orphanage,[2] helps us to see the problem of selfhood and how essential are human surroundings to the realization of an adequate selfhood. Kamala was actually taken from wolves at an estimated age of eight years along with another child apparently a year and a half old. The younger soon died,

[2] J. A. L. Singh and Robert M. Zingg, *Wolf-Children and Feral Man* (New York: Harper & Brothers, 1942).

but the older one lived on for nine years in the mission orphanage at Midnapore. When Kamala, as the missionaries named her, was taken from the wolves, she could neither stand nor walk, but ran wolflike on all fours. She could not in any wise use her hands for handling. She lapped water like a wolf and would not otherwise drink. She not only could not talk, but showed no inclination to communicate. She shunned humans, preferred darkness to light, ate carrion, and howled in the night after the manner of wolves. In a word, Kamala showed what may happen to an otherwise normal human who is subjected to an exclusive wolf-environing life instead of the human environment usual for the human young.

We may add as to Kamala, that though apparently normal in ability, her bad start made her unusually slow in acquiring human traits. She was more than a year in the orphanage before she made her first observed approach to a smile, and for the first three years showed no true smiling or laughing. At first she ate her food head down to the plate, like a dog, and lapped the water she drank. It took five years to form the habit of drinking from a glass. At first she went always on four feet; after a year and a half she made her first vain effort to stand on two feet. In another year and a half she could definitely stand on two feet; in two more years she could walk slowly, but if in a hurry would regularly drop back to all fours. At first, when hungry, she would go smelling about; after three years she had four words she could use for communication; in three more years she was using small sentences. By the time of her death, aged seventeen, she had forty-five words in her vocabulary. It was only after five years at the orphanage that she first went voluntarily to the bathroom to urinate. In short, her whole career shows how essential for normal human life it is to grow up actually among normal people. Neither heredity, to say it scientifically, nor the possession of an immortal soul, to say it theologically, nor innate human nature, to say it as Aristotle saw it—no one of these taken by itself nor all three put together sufficed to give this wolf-child the selfhood that she would have naturally acquired in normal home life.

What do we mean by selfhood? For we must in our thinking distinguish selfhood from the human ability to walk on two feet, for example, or drink from a glass. An ape can learn to do either. For answer—to anticipate the further discussion—we may say that any ordinary child has achieved a working degree of selfhood when

(1) he can distinguish himself from others by the appropriate use of such pronouns as *I, me, mine, you, yours, he, him, his*;

(2) he recognizes himself as an agent, as one who can effect; perhaps using such sentences as: "I didn't do it, Mary did," "I can do it. Let me do it all by myself";

(3) he has achieved a sense of time, past, present, and future, with a notion of his own continuity therein;

(4) he has built a sense of conscious intent and can feel both accountability and responsibility.

HOW SELFHOOD IS ACHIEVED

No baby has these abilities at birth. No lower animal achieves them (except perhaps that under human tutelage certain animals may show a trace of seeming accountability). And this wolf-child had none of them when she was taken at the presumed age of eight from the wolf den. In other words, self-hood is not born in us, and it does not come simply by "maturation" (as the psychologists use the term). It must, as Kamala showed, be achieved by learning under adequate human guidance.

The child achieves his selfhood, we must believe, necessarily in association with other persons who have already achieved it. Selfhood is here understood as that construction, that organization of experiences, out of which the self thinks and acts. It is in fact in process of building all through one's learning life; but it reaches, we may say, a definite stage of effective functioning not long after the child has attained fair ability to talk. The spiritual qualities the race has been accumulating all these years constitute the basis of human family living. The child lives them by participating in the family life. The process goes slowly at first. As the child naturally makes into a milk bottle his varied milk-bottle experiences, so he makes things out of his experiences with those moving objects which are called persons. Names help here by giving distinctions and continuity. Soon the child begins to see that he (his body) is one among those interesting moving things. He sees himself, "from the outside," as having hands and fingers and feet like little sister's. When she falls and cries, mother helps him to understand that it hurts her on the inside just as his fall yesterday hurt him. Out of a thousand such experiences he gradually builds his mind, his personality, his character; and he does this in the give-and-take of associated living in such way that he comes to understand himself in terms of what he sees in others and to understand others in terms of what he sees in himself. His constructed conceptions respectively of his own self and of others (as of like being with him) thus emerge together in his experience, each helping the other into existence. And each such construct as thus formed is compounded of both "self" and "other" elements. Each construct, the resulting self and the resulting other, is a compounded self-other being. The child is accordingly able to see itself more or less truly as others see it and to understand the other, more or less truly, in terms of itself. It is this compounded self-other character of selfhood which makes the human individual able to feel and live the desired spiritual values.

A being able to see itself as others see it and understanding these others in terms of itself has achieved what we may for short call self-consciousness. A dog trying to catch a cat is, we must believe, conscious of the cat but is not in any full sense conscious of itself as running after the cat. True enough, if his mistress has whipped him for running after her cat, he may if mistress comes in sight begin to think of his past whippings as connected with the cat. Thus close may a dog—under human direction—come to self-consciousness. The degree of his self-consciousness, however, falls far below the normal self-consciousness of the human who has achieved normal selfhood.

It is from his use of self-consciousness that the child learns first agency and then accountability. As he learns what he can do, that he can at will effect certain things, he becomes self-conscious of his new skill and is almost certain to wish to show it to others. "Look," he will say, "see me tie my shoe." Later —having achieved a truer measure of agency—he finds that mother and father and others hold him to account for what he does. "Who spilled this salt on the tablecloth?" mother asks, and Mary says, "John did it." As John experiences disapproval for doing forbidden things, he enters a new domain of thought and act.

Morton Prince is quoted as saying "the infant begins his life a thief, impelled by the instinct of greed to grab whatever he sees." The words *thief* and *greed* do not belong in the infant's beginning life but only later when self-other selfhood has been achieved. As soon as the child can use his hands for picking up, he will pick up whatever is in reach. But he cannot be called a thief until he has learned of *property* and the difference between *mine* and *yours* and knowing the difference *willingly* ignores it. All four italicized words are possible only to one who has achieved that much selfhood. The same is true of *greed*. Accountability is built in the child after or as he achieves agency, but not before, and will be built only as the older ones around him have themselves achieved accountability and demand it of him.

Following agency and accountability may come responsibility; but again not the other way about, nor probably here unless his elders show him the way and encourage him in it.

And the encouragement itself depends on the self-other out-look and proceeds in terms of it, that he is pleased when his acts bring approval. Responsibility as a virtue is not fully effected (under any given set of circumstances) until the individual builds in himself his personal approval for doing what other competent ones (as we elders say) approve in him. It is this complex back-and-forth of self and other which explains why responsibility usually follows some while later than agency and accountability.

Moral conflict and conscience, it appears, can come only after obediences to recognized rule have been established in child life; and both depend on a further distinction among what we may call "partial selves," the "internal self" and the "internal other." Imagine a child tempted to do what his mother has forbidden. He might talk thus with himself:

"She said not touch it."

"I will touch it if I want to."

"She said good little boys mind their mother."

"I will touch it; she won't know."

Here we have an internal conflict. One interest, one partial self, the "internal self," inclines him to handle the vase. But a contrary partial self, an "internal other" (representing the absent mother), tells him not to touch it. A beginning sense of *ought* struggles with the natural inclination to handle and examine. So stated, it is a moral conflict; and the child does right or wrong according as the "higher" wins over the "lower." How to tell higher from lower, we must consider; here we assume the superior knowledge of a competent adult. The process of choosing means that one partial self wins out consciously over the other. As the child develops, there will in time normally come feelings during any moral struggle to reinforce one side or the other. Those feelings which accompany attention to recognized authority in connection, and therein stress oughtness, we put in a class by themselves and call conscience or the voice of conscience. Further discussion of conscience will be presented in a moment.

SELFHOOD AND SPIRITUAL VALUES

We have seen enough of the self-other nature of selfhood to recognize its pertinence as a factor in our discussion of spiritual values. The spiritual values are virtually those which have passed through the self-other furnace. At any rate, only those values which have the self-other character are spiritual.

We conclude that only a self-other type of being can build conscious ideals and standards, use critical thinking and language appropriate thereto, and otherwise manifest spiritual quality and choose spiritual values. And this self-other selfhood is, as with the wolf-child Kamala, not an original endowment but an individual achievement, individual in the sense that each one must himself achieve it (as Kamala did not during the eight years of her wolf life). It is not, however, simply an individual achievement. No child achieves it except under the guiding care of those who, profiting by the race achievement, embody in themselves and in their living make manifest more than any individual human living alone (supposing he could keep himself alive) could in his individual lifetime accomplish. From others one learns language and accountability and responsibility and conscience. Only so can selfhood be learned at all.

It is the active possession of such a socially developed self-other selfhood which calls for and constitutes the peculiar dignity of human personality. Kamala had no such actual dignity when she was taken from the wolves. It was her potential selfhood and personality which made it morally obligatory upon the Midnapore missionaries to care for her from the first; just as it is the same potential personality which (aside from our natural love) obligates parents to care for new-born babes. This potential dignity carries obligation because our experience of actual selfhood has set the pattern.

HISTORIC ORIGIN OF THE HIGHER CULTURE

Different people will of course analyze the higher culture in different ways. The seven heads named below seem to us perhaps the most important lines along which civilization has developed, granting the prior advances already named.

1. Moral advance. Before history opens, the beginning foundations of moral conduct had already been everywhere laid. No tribe has been found anywhere at any time so primitive as not to consider and observe its understanding of moral or "good" conduct within its own membership.

2. Enriching the quality of living. Similarly before the dawn of history man had everywhere begun to enrich his life, not only by adorning his useful implements and possessions, but also by the use of poetry, music, and dancing in his celebrations and festivities of all kinds as well as by the pictorial representation of objects in surrounding life that interested him.

3. Respect for personality as such. This came later. Many groups early learned, under compulsion we may suppose, to grant greater respect to the chiefs and nobles in comparison with the commonalty as well as to masters in preference to slaves or other underlings. It seems to have been the Egyptians who about 3500 B.C. first consciously rose above respect for status and conceived respect for the individual as such—respect for personality regardless of status.

4. Conscious criticism. It was the Greeks, it seems, who first in significant degree achieved cultural self-consciousness and thus developed that critical thinking which constitutes the foundation of philosophy and science as we now value them.

5. The Hebraic-Christian tradition. In this was included the idea of one God with man's obligation of absolute obedience to Him, immortality, the conception that sin is inner attitude

(as well as outer act), the duty to love one's fellow as one's self. All these and more, along with their explicit emphasis on the human individual as such, Christianity has spread abroad with profound effect especially on Western civilization.

6. Modern science. This, standing on the Greek foundation, began during the fifteenth and sixteenth centuries to build itself on the verification of hypothesis in actual experience as its only means for establishing validity to thought. The result through the centuries has proved a principal factor to give its distinctive character to modern times.

7. Conscious progress. In the eighteenth century man for the first time got a clear conception of social progress. Two factors seemed especially to enter into this progress: modern thought founded on science and criticism, and a humanitarian outlook (modern democracy) founded on respect for personality and the needed equality of opportunity.

THE CONCEPTION OF THE GOOD LIFE: DEFINITION AND FUNCTION

In any discussion of spiritual values the conception of the good life, of the life good to live, stands strategic. This conception furnishes the foundation of ethics, democracy, and education, defining as it does both the content and the desired goal. Moral obligation, as we now see it, is the obligation so to live and act as to bring the good life at its best possible to all concerned; democracy is the effort to run society on the basis of such an ethics by allowing and requiring people to manage their own collective life; education is leading the young most effectively to live and learn the good life. Mankind has, we believe, made progress toward knowing and living the good life by actual experience and by criticizing the results. It is on the basis of such an inductive study of life as lived that we of this book propose to found our public school pursuit of spiritual values.

The word *good* in the phrase *the good life* is not the moral

good but the consummatory good, that is, good for its purpose. This good life is the life good for living purposes, as a
good apple is an apple good to eat, good music is music good
to hear. It takes the best thought and insight and conscience
we can give to determine what line of conduct in any particular
instance best makes for the good life of all concerned. When
and in so far as we can find out what line of conduct does best
make for the good life of all concerned, in so far we know
what to do. By definition of the term we can say that this fixes
the moral obligation of that situation, namely, so to act as to
bring the good life to all concerned.

It is next important to note more closely the role of deliberation in seeking to establish the path of moral duty. Deliberation
becomes necessary when goods or wants conflict and the better
choice is not obvious. If I face such a conflict, in order to choose
wisely I must widen the range of consideration. I may wisely
take up each possible alternative and ask regarding it, "If I do
this, what will happen? What will be the consequences to all
concerned?" Then I must weigh these different sets of consequences against each other, asking myself, "Which is the set
to choose? Which set shall I back? Which bet my life and
character on? Which adopt as my way of living, considering
the effect on others and also the character effect on myself?"
This seems the actual process of moral choice.

As I do so choose to follow one alternative in preference
to the others, I am in fact choosing what I count to be the good
life for me as this involves the good life for others. If I am a
low-type person (as previously defined), I may choose with
slight weighing of possible future regrets or of other persons.
In the degree that I choose morally, as here conceived, I
choose the line of conduct which promises best for all concerned with no special advantage to myself; and I do this
because in my heart I wish the best for all and am unwilling
myself to profit at the expense of others. And, further, in the
degree that I am morally developed, a feeling of *ought* accom-

panies and ensues from the search and seizes me with a sense of obligation to act upon that alternative which critical study shows to promise best. Before I found out this promising best, I had—if I am truly moral—already committed myself to that course of action which adequate study would disclose as promising best. Thus when a clear judgment is made I feel that I *ought* to follow it. In all of this I am seeking the good life for all concerned. My conception of the good life thus logically and in experience defines for me the object of moral obligation. It is equally true that I am under supreme moral obligation to define as adequately as I can the character of the good life.

SOME CONSTITUENTS OF THE GOOD LIFE

It may help to name some of the constituents of the good life as criticism seems to establish it, partly to make the conception itself clearer, partly to make clearer the distinction between non-spiritual goods and spiritual values, partly to suggest some spiritual values for later service.

Bodily health is a necessary element in the good life but is itself not to be counted a spiritual value. Healthy appetites add to the joy of living and so are morally defensible. But we can well agree with Aristotle that physical appetites should be subordinated to other and "higher" constituents of the good life.

Mental health, the well-adjusted personality, is basic to much if not most of good living. A sense of "security," for example, is obviously a potent factor; without it one is too distraught for either happy or effective living. So also is the proper functioning of personality, which is almost the definition of personality adjustment, necessary to any satisfactory or effective living. How the past has failed to regard these demands for mental health appears in the all-too-frequent school custom of demanding the same of a whole class, so that the lower third has too often been driven into inner rebellion or inferiority complex by the impossible attempt to keep up with the others. Surely this is a positive sin against childhood. Although mental health is vitally important to the good life, it is not properly to be classed among the spiritual values. This kind of health, it appears, is largely shaped in childhood before the child can properly chose. Many maladjustments come in the vain effort of childhood to meet the demands of parents and other elders. The unfortunate victim is at that early age hardly free to decide his own fate.

Perhaps the most strategic of spiritual aims or values is the shaping of such a selfhood—such a mind and character—as is adequate to freedom of choice. Such a degree of selfhood is an achievement over and beyond the initial achieving of ordinary selfhood. To become free to choose in any adequate degree means building the habits (1) of acting on thinking (and not on mere impulse), (2) of holding the mind in suspense until a critical choice can be achieved, (3) of foreseeing consequences (based on accumulated experiences thoughtfully appraised), (4) of weighing sets of possible consequences against each other, (5) of acting out the choice decided upon. And all these overlapping habits must be built into that seamless web of interpenetrating habits we call character.

To build such a character is indeed an achievement—a never-ending task. It means the progressive elimination of prejudice, for prejudice exactly means that some prior decision now holds blindly.

It means, further, not acting simply on custom. "With the savage custom is a blind king," and many far removed from savagery still fail in this respect. It means, in fact, doing everything possible to give free play to intelligence so that this can decide, on merit and nothing else, what is to be done.

To hold thus the free play of intelligence as our final resource to tell us what to do is a source of trouble to some. To them the following may be said. First of all, intelligence is not simply innate, as some seem to hold, but is partly innate and partly constructed through experience out of the social inheritance. It is the second factor here which gives the modern mind its great advantage over the stone age *homo sapiens* who took 25,000 years to improve his flint axe. To rely thus on the free play of intelligence does not mean to reduce life solely to the intellectual. Thinking, the effective use of intelligence, must deal with the complete content of life including prior experience which may be pertinent to the matter at hand. This content of life may be as material as stone or steel; it may be as spiritual as a hope, or a fancy, or a sense of duty. Some hopes are feasible to pursue, others not; thinking—based on pertinent and adequate data—must decide. The same is true for fancies and for impulses to duty. Not all impulses felt as duties can be obeyed. They may conflict; and a particular impulse to duty may be mistaken. Again, it is for thinking to decide.

Still others are troubled as to whether the individual is to be his own judge in the thinking or deciding that he does. Is each one free to think simply as he pleases? The answer to this question is *no*. Thinking that merely follows wish is not thinking in any proper sense. Thinking to deserve acceptance must follow meanings honestly sought and got inherently from the situation as this is seen in the light of previous pertinent and thorough study. Instead one's mere individual judgment— that taken by itself and without further consideration—does not suffice. One is morally bound not to be satisfied with a conclusion that he does not honestly believe would be independently upheld by further impartial study, as competent as his or better. Truth is no private matter, nor is it merely man-made. It is man-contrived, but contrived from what is honestly found. All thinking must fit the whole range of pertinent facts. Strictly speaking, man is free to think only what the facts impartially studied will admit or demand.

The freedom of choice here assumed calls for explanation,

although the discussion on the self-other character of selfhood has already laid sufficient foundation. Some scientific psychologists have tried to treat human behavior without using the conceptions of conscious action or self-consciousness. In the judgment of the makers of this book, this is an indefensible position. The whole range of distinctively human behavior depends on the conception of conscious choosing. This is in no sense a denial of the "principle of causation." "The foreknowledge of possible consequences is," as Herrick points out, "a true causative factor in determining what I shall do."[3]

The freedom of choice is thus not born in us, but achieved, first in achieving selfhood as earlier discussed, then in building adequate habits of choosing as above set out. Freedom of choice means, strictly speaking, freedom to think as thinking has just been described. Different thinking outcomes will mean different resulting conduct. It is in this sense that men are morally free.

A quotation from John Caird may bring to an end this phase of the discussion on freedom to choose.

In the idea of a spiritual, as distinguished from a merely natural being, is involved the notion not only of self-consciousness but of self-determination. Not what I am or find myself to be by nature, nor what I am made to be by any foreign or external power, constitutes my spiritual life, but that which by conscious activity and will, I make myself to be. This does not imply that a spiritual nature is one which is absolutely self-created, or that the spiritual life of the individual has no limits or conditions imposed upon it from without. But it does imply that, so long as there is anything within or without—any element of my inner life which is simply and immediately given, and not taken up, transformed, and, so to speak, recreated by the free self-assertion of the rational will, any outward conditions which constitute a limit to my nature, and which have not become the means of its self-development and self-realization— so long and to that extent I have not attained to the true life of the spirit.[4]

[3] C. Judson Herrick, *Fatalism or Freedom* (New York: Norton, 1926), pp. 61f.

[4] John Caird, *An Introduction to the Philosophy of Religion* (Glasgow: James Maclehose, 1901), pp. 247f.

Associated living may next be stressed as an essential element in the good life, indeed, the principal factor in calling our spiritual values into active being. To live in community is clearly necessary to living the good life. Without this, to begin with, no one would be born; and if born, he would soon die. Without this, no one would achieve normal human personality, even if he could be kept alive. Without this human association, to readapt Hobbes's words, "the life of man [would be] solitary, poor, nasty, brutish, and short." Certainly, associated living is a definite good, an aggregate of goods.

Out of associated living come many—some would say all —of our spiritual values. So far as history and anthropology can show, morals began as the mores, the folkways, the varied trial-and-error solutions, of the tribal group to the problem of living better in close company with others. Thus is derived a sense of common effort directed toward common ends. The proper conduct of individuals is thus fixed in the natural give-and-take of associated life. Through the long years certain ways of behaving become so regularized and carry such general recognition and approval that the individual counts upon his responsible fellows to support him in demanding these as "rights." And this of course implies that others are under obligation to respect these "rights," and one is in turn under similar obligation to respect their "rights." Thus "rights" and correlative "duties" emerge simultaneously, each mutually implying the other.

So long as these customs were mere customs and accepted without thought except to obey or enforce them, they had not attained to the level of personal spiritual quality or value. But when, as with the Greeks especially, a variety of cultural contacts at length brought cultural self-consciousness, conscious questioning arose as to which custom was really right, and what right in this sense could mean, and how it could be determined. When out of such questioning men began to see further into the how and why of moral goods, these goods thus criticized became values. In some such way did spiritual values in the fuller sense as here used arise in and for man.

That the spiritual values found in the intellectual and aesthetic realms also thus arose through human association needs but to be stated. Men in interaction mutually stimulated each other to further contributions. The cultural history of man is eloquent with the story. The spiritual values of thought obviously permit us to associate more fully and more reliably with each other. The aesthetic values bring the further keen pleasure of sharing thought and feeling with others. Specifically, science through the objectivity it permits allows men to count more surely on each other as well as more surely on human efforts at control. Art, as we saw earlier, allows the rest of us to share measurably in the recorded "experiences which have seemed worth having to the most sensitive and discriminating persons."

Do these spiritual values, as is here assumed, really mean a richer life to man? Does cultivation of them add to life? Does moral quality add to life? These are proper questions, which we wish next to consider. We may anticipate part of the answer by a statement from George Eliot:

We can only have the highest happiness, such as goes with being a great man, by having wide thoughts, and much feeling for the rest of the world as well as ourselves; and this sort of happiness often brings so much pain with it that we can only tell it from pain by being what we would choose before everything else, because our souls see it as good.[5]

The intellectual and spiritual formulation of the conception of the good life is a philosophy in which one tries to bring together in one inclusive and, if possible, consistent whole what life means in all its bearings and implications. That each one has some outlook on life is implicit if he thinks at all. Each individual as he matures owes it to himself to make such an outlook as inclusive and defensible as he can. Some will ask

[5] George Eliot, *Romola* (Edinburgh: Blackwood, no date), Epilogue, p. 503.

as to relation of this to religion. If with Coe we define religion psychologically, we might say that in the degree one holds his philosophy with living fervor it becomes for him his religion of life. If men generally accepted this point of view and were willing to decide their vital philosophies by study and criticism, the purpose for this book would essentially be met. That such a philosophy would be supreme among the spiritual results of study needs hardly be said.

THE VALIDITY OF SPIRITUAL VALUES

Few questions have recently been more debated than whether and how the received spiritual values are to be defended at the bar of reason. In science men well agree that that hypothesis is to be accepted which best forecasts what outcome to expect. In an earlier day there were those who decried this putting of truth upon the "test of the senses" since, they alleged, we tell by seeing or feeling or hearing whether the outcome prophesied has come true. But men decreasingly question the method of science where it can fairly be used.

There was a time when men thought the method of Euclid the most certain available to man. Hobbes said (1651) of geometry that it is "the only science that it hath pleased God hitherto to bestow on mankind." When Thomas Jefferson in the Declaration of Independence said, "We hold these truths to be self-evident," we may take it that he was following the analogy of axioms in Euclid. But during the nineteenth century it became evident to mathematicians that Euclid's axioms were not self-evident, but were rather assumptions. And at least one of these, that relating to parallel lines, was so far from being self-evident that two contradictory alternatives are additionally conceivable. Out of this situation several independent geometries have in fact been made; and it seems forever impossible by scientific methods to prove the exact truth of Euclid. With the *a priori* approach thus shut out of its ancient castle scientists as such have given it up; and thinkers in general decreasingly use it.

If we go to the other extreme of human interest, the aesthetic, we find it difficult to "prove" acceptable standards. Possibly we should not try. It was said of old that concerning tastes there can be no settlement by argument; and some current disputes in the field would seem to illustrate the point. But in spite of so pessimistic an outlook men do achieve great measures of consensus; and pertinent cultivation seems on the whole to increase consensus. William Shakespeare is thus among mature minds all but unanimously counted superior to Laura Jean Libby. Homer is similarly acclaimed above Whittier, though Whittier is widely enjoyed. The Mona Lisa will, we may well believe, last as an object of true interest longer than most pictures painted in either its century or ours. Rembrandt will please for long if not forever. Few indeed would rank the Albert Memorial above the Parthenon; and it seems now probable that men will forever wonder at the "slump" in taste during that Memorial period. There will, we must suppose, be disputes forever as to the precise names to be included among the truly great in the realm of the aesthetic, but there appear also great agreements. Certainly the matter is not simply arbitrary; though with equal certainty authority in any external sense cannot settle disputes in this area. Moreover, new study may make new distinctions. Even so artistic a people as the Greeks painted their marble statuary and could not surely distinguish the color blue from the color green. Progress is possible and even in the aesthetic realm we do not know what the future may bring forth. But in this realm there appear probable such sweeping advances as have been found in science and technology. In conclusion, consensus among those who cultivate taste does achieve considerable agreement. In this area we can say that, within limits, aesthetic standards are established in the form of the taste of enlightened and cultured persons.

We now return to the moral realm. Is it proper to say that moral quality and moral values have emerged naturally in human history just as have other insights and discoveries in other realms? The answer seems to be yes. In times past when men knew little of history and well-nigh nothing of anthropology, when cultural progress was so slow as to be unnoticeable, it was easy to ascribe not only original moral instruction but the initial knowledge of the mechanical arts to some divine source. Even in the lifetime of men now living it was taught that the Bible is the oldest of books and that other religions than that which it declared are worthy of no comparative respect. But a wider knowledge of other cultures, the doctrine of evolution, a study of comparative religion, the "higher criticism" of the Bible, and a closer study of comparative moralities have brought an increasing conviction that the ideas and standards of human thought and action have a long cultural history and are to be studied as one whole piece, a seamless web of human effort.

What about moral standards? And what is it that gives validity to moral obligation? Must we here appeal to the supernatural? Men differ on the answer; some say yes, others say no. And among those answering no are many who yield to none in their allegiance to their religion, whether it be the Christian, the Jewish, the Buddhist, the Hindu, or the Mohammedan. These say that their religion implies belief in or holds a place for a "natural" order and that morals can be studied as other natural things are studied. Indeed, they go on to say that to put morals on an authoritarian basis would rob them of inherent moral quality to the great loss of the moral outlook.

It seems to the makers of this book best for the public school to treat morals on this inherent basis, to get young people to see how public and private honesty, for example, do make life finer and richer for all concerned; how integrity is in observable fact necessary for any decent living among men.

If these things can be seen as inherently true, true to natural human insight, the probabilities seem to us the more promising that under proper guidance youth will accept them to live them.

We have been examining the origin of morals. We now carry the discussion further into the nature and scope of moral obligation, to see how in fact moral obligation follows the rule of the widest good. Even youth can make a beginning of this insight in their games. They can easily see how team play should overrule and decide individual play; that no player may properly sacrifice or even jeopardize the team victory in order to get glory for himself alone. What selfishness means is easily taught in this connection; it is the willingness to get good for one's self at the expense of an admitted obligation to one's fellows. In an earlier day men spoke of "enlightened selfishness" as the proper rule of life; and some among us even today profess to believe that all men are selfish in all they do. So to think is to be guilty of muddled thinking. Men do act, as they must, each out of himself, out of his own selfhood and character; there is no other way. But such action need not be selfish. The suffix -ish carries a derogatory implication, as is evident when we compare mannish with manly, or woman-ish with womanly. Selfish is the term used to indicate an undue regard for self. The player who sells out the game to show what he as an individual can do is acting selfishly, as youngsters have no trouble in seeing.

The principle goes still further. If a house be afire in a village possessed of no fire system, all citizens must help. They so feel. "My time may come next," they say. But I who have no house, am I still obligated to help? Or what of my obligation if I am a stranger, simply happening along when the fire begins? The answer remains yes. I am still a man; I can feel for the man whose house is threatened; if I can in reason help, I must. This we believe is a good rule. I may never own a house but I do have interests liable to jeopardy. If I should need help, I hope others will come to my aid. If they need help, I must stand ready to help them.

We can perhaps generalize something about values from this discussion. If a rule is a good rule, good when I am caught and others help me, good when others are similarly caught and I help them, and so good a rule that competent judges approve it the more they watch it work, then a principle of moral obligation comes into play. Unless countermanded by stronger principles, I owe it to this man now in trouble to help him if, in reason, I can. Moral obligation comes thus into operation in the degree that we have reason to approve a certain line of conduct as best for all concerned. In this sense, moral obligation holds as far as human sympathy can extend and human effort in reason go.

But there will be those who are not convinced by this argument. What shall we say to them? We disregard here that large number who selfishly refuse to act morally; they present a psychological-educational, not a moral-logical problem. There remain a few who deny the existence of moral obligation or at any rate argue that no proof of such has been given. There remain too that larger number who say that except as we can rely upon some power and authority outside of and beyond human experience we can have neither basis for moral obligation nor reasonable expectation that it can prevail among men as having persuasive influence in their choice of conduct.

It is improbable that any answer, however valid, will at once satisfy all; but some things can be said. The question is, How can we prove the binding power of moral obligation as here described? Proof is a hard word, especially in this area. Perhaps probability is as much as we can expect. There are other areas of life where probability is all we have, but we act on it just the same. In fact, it seems likely that we act at best on probability, direct or indirect. Who can *prove* that this surgical case needs the indicated operation? Even if the patient is operated upon and gets well—or dies—who can *prove* that he would not have got well—or died—without the operation? In such a case, as long as we deal with this patient only, we can perhaps prove nothing. But from a study of similar cases and their outcomes, with and without treatment, we may be able to establish certain probabilities; and it is on these that men act. Every day we do in fact bet our lives and our sacred honor upon such probabilities. Taken directly or indirectly, probability seems all that men have to go on.

Consider now the assumption of the reality of moral obligation that it is binding under the conditions set forth above. The question arises—Do the probabilities based on actual experience uphold this hypothesis? The answer would seem a clear yes. Almost every moral leader, almost every careful student of the question, would so answer. Most practical men would concur for, at any rate, most of the time. The exceptions offered or observed can be studied to see what they show. When so studied, they seem to fall mostly into two groups. One set of seeming great importance is in the area largely of selfish statecraft or the prosecution of war; another set, larger in point of number, in petty trade transactions and the like. But the further study of the conditions underlying these exceptions call in question the social propriety of such statecraft and of war on the one hand, and the social-economic educational conditions operating with the petty offenders on the other. In other words, closer study seems not to move toward invalidating the hypothesis, but rather to upholding it.

In short, the difficulty attending the kind of morals herein upheld is not with the ethical theory or with any innate weakness of normal human nature. The real difficulty lies with the inherent educative effects of unsatisfactory social conditions, including inadequate social arrangements. In the degree that due attention be given to bettering these conditions and arrangements, in like degree, granted the enforcement of proper order and wisely directed education, we may hope for moral improvement. Some social lag will always be present, and evil we shall have with us as long as variety holds in natural affairs. It is only recently, as history goes, that mankind has even conceived of progress. With study increasingly directed to social life and its betterment, it seems not impossible to hope that conscious effort may here as elsewhere bring great moral advance.

Chapter IV

THE SPIRITUAL VALUES OF THE SECULAR PUBLIC SCHOOL

THE SECULAR PATTERN OF AMERICAN PUBLIC EDUCATION

THE American public school is a secular institution. In both its purposes and its patterns of control and administration, it reflects the American democratic tradition of religious liberty and separation of church and state. The public school opens its doors to all the children of the community. It does not seek to indoctrinate the young with any particular body of religious beliefs, or to nurture them in the rituals and ceremonies of any religious sect. It is controlled, not by ecclesiastical authorities, but by lay authorities elected, or appointed, by the civil community. It is maintained, not by gifts from religious or other private agencies, but by public funds derived from taxes levied on the whole community. Finally, it requires no religious test whatever of either its teachers or the members of its administrative boards. Many have long regarded this secular, non-sectarian character of the American public school as a necessary, distinctive, and morally desirable expression of our democratic principles.

At the present time, however, as indicated earlier in this book, certain church groups are seeking to have this secular pattern of our public educational program reviewed and revised. These religious leaders assert that the secularism of the public school constitutes a threat, not only to the churches, but also to the spiritual strength of our democracy. Democracy, they argue, is an ethical way of life as well as a form of government; it is grounded in a fundamental respect for individual human personality; and this respect for the dignity of each and every person depends, in turn, upon the maintenance of faith in a loving, extramundane Supreme Being. Hence the public schools have a responsibility to cultivate in the young those religious appreciations, attitudes, and beliefs which, they hold, constitute the moral foundation of our democratic faith. As one earnest exponent of this point of view states, this proposal may seem to be a denial of our historic principle of religious liberty but actually it is not:

Increasingly the principle of religious liberty is now being seen as a positive principle expressing the need for religious expression as a part of the corporate life of a people. In other words, it means freedom to participate in religious worship and activity—not simply freedom to avoid it. And such freedom can be realized only when the education of the young makes them intelligent about religion and predisposes them toward a positive appraisal of its resources.[1]

The main obstacle in American life to the growth of an effective social ethic is the disease which I have called the secularization of the mind. If that fault is to be remedied our common religious heritage must be recovered in our educational system.[2]

Whatever one may think of the soundness of this demand, it must be recognized that a minority has a moral right and a political obligation to call the attention of the public to questions which it believes have been wrongly decided. Equally, it is an intellectual and civic responsibility in a democratic society for those who favor the perpetuation of an established policy to state frankly and definitely the reasons which prompt them to support it. Certainly for members of the John Dewey Society no existing political or educational practice can be satisfactorily justified by merely pointing to the fact that it is the outcome of a long historical process. For the experimentalist, or functionalist, the supreme and crucial test of a policy or of an institution is not that past experience led to its adoption,

[1] F. Ernest Johnson, *The Social Gospel Re-examined* (New York: Harper & Brothers, 1940), p. 183.
[2] *Ibid.*, pp. 190-191.

or that it is now the law of the land, but rather that its present probable consequences are judged best to promote the common good.

One purpose of this book is to state the grounds for our conviction that there is no opposition between the present secular public school and the conservation and cultivation of spiritual interests in American life. We do not believe that the American people are forced to choose between the present public school pattern and practice, on the one hand, and the preservation of the spiritual values inherent in our democratic heritage, on the other. On the contrary, we regard the public school, in spite of its present inadequacies, as one of the most powerful spiritual resources American democracy has on its side in this difficult period of social upheaval and transition.

THE SHIFT FROM CHURCH TO CIVIL COMMUNITY

Even if the record of the past cannot in and of itself determine what policy the public school should now adopt, it does, however, provide a perspective from which the problem of spiritual values and education can be fruitfully examined. It is clear from this record that it is the American people, not the public school teachers, who are primarily responsible for whatever "secular" character our educational system now has. Indeed, the American public school in its origin, organization, control, and program is probably our supreme illustration of the democratic conception that an institution should be of, by, and for the people. This public school system was neither created by federal legislation nor designed by any central planning agency. Its present pattern and practice is the result of an organic growth in which the interests, the purposes, and the initiative of the people have played the primary role. Both its support and its control have been predominantly state and local, not national. And in the various states and local communities arrangements have been devised to keep the educational authorities directly responsible to the people whose children are in the schools, not to remote government officials.

The public school system is also designed to serve *all* the people. It is committed to the principle of equality of opportunity at all levels of its program. The teachers are representative of the community in which they work. Many of them are the products of its homes. They share its interests, outlooks, sentiments, and aspirations. Parents regard them as fellow members of the community, not as officials of an external authority. To a remarkable extent the school is accepted as an institution of the neighborhood, sharing with the homes in the care and nurture of the children. Our public schools are open to visitation by parents and interested citizens as is true apparently of no other country in the world.

Although the public schools are locally controlled and administered, and the schools of each community or state have their individualized features, they also exhibit in remarkable degree certain common aims and principles of practice. In spite of explicit control by forty-eight separate states and measurable control by innumerable local districts the public schools of our country, viewed collectively, may properly be said to constitute a national system. But this "system" is the product of a common American way of life and thought—no external agency has designed and imposed it upon a reluctant people.

In the course of its development, public education in the United States has undergone important changes. One of the most important has been the gradual shift from the ecclesiastical and religious pattern of the colonial and early national period to the civic and secular pattern of our time. This shift involved modifications in the aims of the school, in curriculum, in the part played by church and clergy in the control of the school, in the sources of material support, and in both the agencies and the criteria of certification of teachers. These changes have been going on for over a century, in certain respects they have occurred at different times in different sections of the country, and even today public policy and practice concerning them are not wholly uniform throughout the country.

At times sharp controversies about the interrelations of religion and education arose, and appeals were taken to the legislatures and courts for rulings on points about which the local and state communities were divided. In some instances special provisions were even introduced into state constitutions in order to define the relation of the church and religion to public education. The outcome after a century of experience, discussion, and experiment was the acceptance of the civic and, with some qualifications, the secular pattern for the public schools.

A generation ago many assumed that this was one issue which the American people had finally settled. This conviction that history had returned a verdict to the effect that public education in the United States was a function of the state, not the church, and that its program was to be civic and secular in character is clearly the dominant note in a historical study made by Dr. Brown and published in 1912 under the revealing title: *The Secularization of American Education.* He summarizes his findings as follows:

The foregoing citations from laws, from constitutional provisions, and from judicial decisions portray rather definitely some of the more important phases of a process which has been going on in this country for something over a hundred years, the secularization of education.

The laws cited, which bear dates prior to 1776, and occasionally one within the early national period, show as a rule the close connection of church and school, or religion and education during the colonial days and the early years of the republic. They show the largely religious aim of education, the largely religious nature of the subject matter of instruction, and the considerable part played by the church in the control of schools. They show the state beginning to recognize the importance of education for her own welfare and beginning to contribute to the support thereof, but leaving unto the church a large measure of control in the supervision and administration of schools.

In the laws and constitutional provisions enacted subsequent to about

1850, following an intervening period devoted largely to local legislation, in which there is state legislation relating to religion and education in but few states, we see the preponderance of the church in educational affairs supplanted by that of the state. The dominant aim of the school becomes a civic one, the subject matter of instruction is purged of everything savoring of sectarian or denominational religious nature, and control shifts from the church and her ministry to the state and her officials. Control of education becomes largely centralized, uniform series of text-books and courses of study are provided for, provision is made for state and county certification of teachers, and all forms of religious tests for teachers or school officials are forbidden. Most of the constitutional provisions have to do with safeguarding the school revenues, derived from permanent funds and taxation, against diversion to contending religious educational claimants, and with protecting the schools themselves from the zeal of contending religious sects, who have sought from time to time to use the public agencies of instruction for the propagation of their own peculiar tenets.

In no less than thirty-five states has there been enacted specific legislation or constitutional provisions against either sectarian religious instruction or the use of text-books containing sectarian religious material, in state supported schools. While usually the prohibition has been confined in the enactments to "sectarian religion," yet practically this has come to mean all religious instruction.[3]

Dr. Brown also gives us his analysis of the factors that operated to bring about this momentous change in the plan of American public education:

So it has come to pass that necessity has led the state to provide for education; and sectarian differences have made it necessary that this education should be non-sectarian or non-religious. . . . While the non-religious elements have no doubt frequently allied themselves with the movement toward secularization, yet it can hardly be said that they have been the controlling factor therein. Differences of religious belief and a sound regard on the part of the state for individual freedom in religious matters, coupled with the necessity of centralization and uniformity, rather than hostility toward religion as such, lie at the bottom of the movement toward the secular school.[4]

[3] S. W. Brown, *The Secularization of American Education* (New York: Teachers College, Columbia University, 1912), pp. 155-156.
[4] *Ibid.*, p. 3.

Dr. Brown is right in emphasizing that it was not "hostility toward religion as such" which explains this gradual acceptance of the secular pattern. It is clear, as he indicates, that the presence of sectarian and denominational divisions in the United States was one important factor which helped to produce "the movement toward the secular school."

Denominational rivalry was probably not, however, the chief influence which accounts for the shift from the church and ecclesiastical to the civic pattern in American education. It appears that a deeper and more powerful cause of this shift was the secularist trend in Western civilization which had been gathering momentum for several centuries. The roots of this secularist movement lie in scientific, political, moral, and religious developments in process for centuries, and which are now part of the warp and woof of our modern democratic and scientific culture. It was because this secularist attitude and emphasis were becoming dominant in our society that it eventually gained ascendancy in the public school. On the whole, I believe these so-called "secular" developments are deeply spiritual in character. Taken together these changes have resulted in a movement more in harmony with the moral and spiritual interests of democracy than are the traditional outlooks and the political, social, and educational arrangements which they supplanted. In the writer's opinion, to return to the former would be to lower, not to raise, the spiritual quality of American life and education.

AUTHORITY AND FREEDOM OF THOUGHT

One of the earliest demands of the secularist movement was for freedom of thought. This took the form of the desire to free from supernatural and authoritarian presuppositions the process by which knowledge is achieved. It advocated the right of the inquirer to follow the lead of his subject matter and thought without arbitrary limitation from any established authority—ecclesiastical, military, or political. In sum, it demanded the recognition of the autonomy of the realm of knowledge. It believed that experience—equipped with the methodology of experimental science—should stand on its own foundations. It first contended for the recognition of this right in the discovery and testing of ideas in the physical or natural sphere, later it demanded that this empirical pattern of inquiry be universalized and applied also to the human and moral sphere.

The basic presupposition of this secular demand for the recognition of the autonomy of the sphere of knowledge is the conviction that all knowledge is developed by human beings, and is not to be had either by immediate intuition or by any process of supernatural revelation. Recognizing that ordinary human beings are inevitably involved in the process by which all beliefs are discovered, tested, reconstructed, and established, secularism is here concerned with the means by which this human process can be so conducted and controlled that it will yield reliable or warranted conclusions. Its primary insight is that this can be achieved only as the process of knowledge becomes a co-operative undertaking in which each person so conducts his inquiry that he can make available to others a description of the conditions in which it originated, a record of what he did and what happened, and a summary of the conclusions he draws from his investigation.

Obviously this requires that the experimental situation be an empirical one with its terms and procedures so definite and objective that they can be reproduced and checked by others competent in the given field of investigation. By this insistence on shareable conditions and practices, as well as on public records open to all who may be interested, experimental science provided against the operation of arbitrary "subjective" or "individualistic" biases which preclude the possibility of gaining common meanings and conclusions. Thus, knowledge, through the socialization of the method by which it is attained, is saved from the limited perspectives, blind spots, prejudices, arbitrary hunches, and intuitions of the individual and so made far more reliable than by any alternative measures yet conceived. By recognizing the hypothetical or tentative character of all such empirically established beliefs, research science escapes dogmatism and provides for the revision of any and all its findings through its own established practices. By this free, socialized procedure the way is kept open for experimenters—even those of generations as yet unborn—to detect and overcome the errors of those who have preceded them.

Whatever man can enjoy in the way of objectivity in knowledge, or truth, is thus dependent upon this co-operative, experimental method. "Secularism" is the social movement which sought to win public support for this method. Its insistence on freedom of thought and the autonomy of the sphere of knowledge was the social and political counterpart of its insight into the conditions essential for gaining knowledge, and of the need of protecting the community of inquirers from outside interferences which would hinder or destroy the only process by which an uncoerced consensus can be attained. Obviously an ethical implication of the highest import is involved in this public, experimental process of inquiry, and the spiritual heritage of the race was enriched by its development.

In time this empirical methodology was made an important part of the education of the young. Both the findings of science and the methods and techniques of science become dominant in many phases of the curriculum of the school. This emphasis on free inquiry and empirical proof was in deep conflict with older authoritarian and supernatural presuppositions. As Horace Mann and others emphasized, it would be difficult to nurture these two contrasting outlooks in one and the same educational program.

In so far as the leaders of the church resisted this empirical pattern on the assumption that religious meanings and values depended upon the maintenance of the earlier conceptions of knowledge and its means, they were opposed to a deep-moving tendency in modern culture. It is not surprising that the people of the country, habituated as they were by their everyday experience to the practices of science and technology, gradually came to favor the secular pattern of freedom of thought for the public school. They were committed by everyday affairs and practices to empirical outlooks and procedures even though many did not recognize all of the philosophical and theological implications and consequences of this commitment.

In the opinion of the writer, the introduction of this non-authoritarian, experimental, co-operative procedure into the school was an ethical action. It has strengthened, not weakened, the spiritual life of our people.

THE DECLINE OF SUPERNATURALISM

The secularist trend was further strengthened by profound transformations which were taking place in the utilitarian activities, the intellectual interests, and the moral life of man. The rise of modern science greatly extended the range of man's intellectual and practical activities. Many phases of both his physical and social surroundings, long ignored or minimized, now become absorbing objects of exploration. No aspect of human experience—soil fertilization, animal breeding, road building, disease-breeding germs, the invention and improvement of machines, the making of goods—was now considered too common or mean to serve as subject matter for serious study. The scientific study of the structure and behavior of living creatures, including the human organism, yielded bodies of fact and insight into processes which had long been supposed to lie beyond the range of mere human understanding.

The application of science to the ways of making a living also contributed new powers of control over the physical environment. It made many new materials available for human use and opened up sources of energy hitherto unutilized. These technological advances called for readjustments in the ways of living and for the reconstruction of many ancient institutionalized practices. Man became accustomed to change, and began to look upon it as the normal possibility of human progress and improvement, not as a sign of the decay of an already perfected social life.

Indeed, these revolutionary developments in both the practical and the intellectual life began to breed a new temper and outlook in Western man. The world of tradition, speculation, fable, and symbol began to give way before the new world of nature and fact which science was disclosing; the traditional sense of the wickedness or weakness of man and of the evil of the world was replaced by growing faith in human intelligence and a sturdy respect for human individuality; other-worldly preoccupations were supplanted by interest in the vivid possibilities of the here and now, and dependence upon supernatural powers and docile submission to established arrangements were superseded by a fresh confidence in man's creative power and the possibility of achieving a more meaningful life than the race had as yet experienced.

Under the influence of new scientific discoveries and evolutionary conceptions older dualisms of man and nature, mind and body, the spirit and the flesh, ends and means, the intellectual and the practical, the cultural and the vocational, the good and goods, the divine and the human began to disappear. Man was increasingly viewed as an emergent within the world of nature, not as a ghostly substance inserted from another order of being.

This developing secularist outlook did not involve, for probably most of the people, the rejection of belief in personal immortality, but it did definitely result in a changed orientation in which the practical autonomy of affairs in this world was widely accepted. The enjoyments, the meanings, the resources and possibilities of the present were no longer subordinated to the alleged requirements of life in another world. The principle of ascetic renunciation as a means of spiritual preparation for a future existence was abandoned, as was the notion that harsh and unjust conditions of living should be accepted with passive resignation because of their supposed disciplinary value. Belief in personal immortality was widely retained, but it was now commonly believed that the best possible preparation for that existence which lay beyond the grave was the most useful and meaningful life in the present. Future salvation was no longer regarded as an acceptable alternative to a satisfactory present experience.

Not only was the value and dignity of man's life in this world increasingly recognized, but in one department of human affairs after another lay groups began to assume control over activities long under the direction of the church. Both the ends these activities were seeking to promote and the means by which these ends were to be attained were progressively determined by those directly responsible for them. Thus, today, farmers plant and harvest their crops, industrialists organize their production, merchants regulate their buying and selling, workers organize their unions, legislators enact laws, social workers care for delinquents and dependents, artists paint pictures, dramatists write plays, and parents care for their children without recourse to supernatural sanctions or authoritative direction from the church. This does not mean that the ethical insights derived from our religious tradition are inoperative in these various fields, but it does mean that lay men and women, responding to developing conditions of life, now determine the particular relevance this ethical tradition has for the various departments of life in which they are engaged.

Experience has shown this specialization can be carried to extremes—functional lay groups can degenerate into narrow pressure groups unmindful of the larger community good. Specialized departments may fail in their co-ordination with one another, and conflicts may result which injure the community as a whole. The need for more effective means to provide for co-operation and responsible attention to the general welfare on the part of these various functional groups is acute at the present time, but few today even suggest that it should be met by returning these activities to the moral control of the clergy. This co-ordinating and supervisory function has passed to the government and seems destined to remain under secular, civil control. The heart of the present dispute is about the manner in which the state should be reorganized so that it may more adequately discharge its growing responsibilities in our interdependent industrial society. It is not about the desirability of returning the functions of the state to a religious agency and authority.

To this extent at least, secularism has become the common presupposition of the modern world.

THE NEW CURRICULUM OF THE PEOPLE'S SCHOOL

The increasing secularization of modes of life and thought outside the school had its important consequences for the aims and program of the school. The expansion of the number and variety of human interests, the increasing appreciation of the values inherent in present human experience, the growth of systematic bodies of knowledge in many specialized fields, and the new and powerful position of lay groups in modern society resulted in a this-worldly attitude which radically altered the emphasis and content of the school program. The subject matter of the school was no longer primarily drawn from religious and literary classics; it was progressively found in fields of knowledge and activity which were playing a dominant part in the life of modern man. Gradually it became recognized that the primary work of the school was to equip the young to take their full part in these ongoing affairs of the community, not to introduce them to the beliefs of supernatural religion or to the ceremonies of the church. Even the schools which continued to be supported and controlled by the churches radically changed their emphasis and program in order to maintain vital contact with the developing life of society now so deeply "secular" in mood and institutionalized practice.

The conception and pattern of character education was likewise profoundly modified. The quality of the character of the individual came to be judged by his ability to take a responsible and co-operative part in the affairs of family, civic, vocational, and social life. The school continued to carry responsibility for the development of character, but more adequate knowledge about the actual process by which habits and attitudes are developed makes it less and less inclined to emphasize special courses in morals. Good conduct is increasingly viewed as a product of responsible participation in the daily activities of the group.

This changing human temper also found expression in modified methods of teaching. Dogmatic, catechetical, and *memoriter* methods were progressively supplanted by inductive empirical procedures. The former type of method may be appropriate when teaching is viewed as the induction of the young into a supernatural pattern of life and salvation which must be imposed from above because the young have no means of acquiring it through the processes of ordinary human experience and reflection. But these methods of demonstration from fixed first principles do not harmonize with the mind-set of a society increasingly committed to the principles of democracy and the methods of experimental science. Hence in the public schools the program was gradually changed so that less emphasis was given to authoritarian inculcation, and more provision was made for the child to develop ideas in connection with firsthand experiences with things and persons.

The curriculum was redesigned to provide greater opportunity for learning from observation of nature, from actual experience with community affairs, and from meaningful group activities organized within the school. Respect for human personality was interpreted to involve respect for the interests and experiences of the child, and education was viewed as a process of reconstruction of experience carried on under the guidance of teachers who were concerned that the child should understand that which he learned, not merely accept things on the basis of adult authority. To be sure, these newer conceptions of method have by no means won universal acceptance in the public schools, but both the methods of science and the ideals of democracy have combined to give growing support to the more experiential and non-authoritarian school procedures.

These tendencies in the "secular" culture were also reflected in the processes by which teachers are educated, certified, and appointed. As new fields of educational activity developed, teachers had to have special qualifications to work in them. These areas of educational specialization were organically connected with the rapidly developing autonomous fields of interest in society, such as science, occupations, public services, family life, art, recreation, health, and the like. Gradually teachers came to be examined and appointed to school positions, not primarily because of their knowledge of the traditions and doctrines of the churches, but because of their demonstrated competence in one or more of these specialized fields of educational activity. As the states and their administrative subdivisions progressively assumed responsibility for the granting of teacher licenses, all religious tests for teachers in the public schools were omitted. Thus, by the action of lay groups in the various states and local communities, American public education was finally brought into harmony with the secular principle articulated in the sixth Article of the federal Constitution, which stipulates that "no religious test shall ever be required as a qualification to any office or public trust in the United States."

These two basic changes in the administrative pattern—the certification of teachers by the lay, political authority, and the elimination of religious tests—have done much to make our public educational system in the United States secular in character. Only a people whose ways of life and thought had already been deeply penetrated by secular developments would have been disposed to initiate these transformations in policy for its education of the young in the public schools. They signify a growing consciousness on the part of the people of the essential characteristics of a democratic community, and the pattern of freedom which must be institutionalized in its educational procedures if democracy is to prosper. They also indicate that a shift in the basis of authority has taken place. Controlling ideals and regulative standards of education are now considered to evolve from within the context of ordinary experience itself, not from sources above and beyond the activities by which, and in which, the human group lives, moves, and has its being.

DEMOCRACY AND SECULARISM

Whether these changes in life outlook and practice which are now reflected in the patterns of our secular public school system are to be regarded as spiritual in nature will obviously depend on the meanings one most deeply associates with the term "spiritual." As has been emphasized by many historians, these changes in the aims, program, and control of public education were not made by the American people because they were indifferent or hostile to the interests of spiritual religion. On the contrary, they were moved to secularize public education because of their loyalty to some of the deepest spiritual meanings of American life. In addition to their loyalty to the pattern of experimental science, they regarded democracy, both as a form of government and as a personal and social way of life, as the very core of our ethical and spiritual heritage.

As a form of government, democracy has its secular connotations. It means most basically the rule of the people—the right of self-government. A democratic form of government could only develop in a society which was prepared to lodge sovereignty with the whole people, not with some special order or restricted class of men. This basic faith in the ability of the common man to govern is superbly disclosed in our earliest political document, the Declaration of Independence. It declares:

That all men are created equal,
That they are endowed by their Creator with certain unalienable rights,
That among these are life, liberty and the pursuit of happiness,
That to secure these rights governments are instituted among men,
That governments derive their just powers from the consent of the governed, and
That the people have the right to alter or abolish any form of government which becomes destructive of these human ends.

Manifestly in a society of this type—in which all men are to be considered equal; in which the officials are chosen from the people by means of a system of stated and free elections; in which all enjoy the right to propose and to discuss freely public measures and policies, not excluding those which involve reconstruction of the very forms of the state itself; in which all have a common obligation to accept decisions duly made without resort to force; and in which minorities are protected in their peaceful efforts to make themselves into majorities and to have their views adopted whenever they succeed in gaining popular support—no institution, authority, or leadership, ecclesiastical or otherwise, could be given a preferred status. In so far as any special order were thus granted a privileged position in the processes of government, the doctrine of equality of rights and the sovereignty of the people would to that extent be impaired.

Political democracy with its presupposition of a government which rests on the free consent of all of the governed very definitely implies a society in which the "lay" principle has become universalized. The leaders of the church are citizens with all the rights of citizenship, but their ideas and proposals can become influential only as they win their way in free and open competition with those advanced by other groups of citizens. In other words, in a political democracy clergymen are also laymen along with the rest of the population. In this political sense, the pattern of democracy is essentially and necessarily a secular one. It is therefore a confused and misleading form of thinking which holds that in order to conserve our democratic heritage we must abandon this secular principle. To abandon it would mean the destruction of one of the essentials of the democratic way of life.

But American democracy is not only a form of government, it is also a personal and a social way of life. As a mode of individual and group life, democracy has its positive moral meanings. The social-democratic conception affirms that each and every person is worthy of respect and is never to be treated as a mere means for the advancement of the interests of others. It holds that respect for the concrete human individual necessarily involves respect for his capacities, interests, preferences, and ideas. This also involves recognition of his right, in cooperation with his fellows, to shape and reshape the institutions of his community. Moreover, according to the principles of social democracy, institutions are means; individuals are ends. The ultimate test of any institution is what it contributes to the enrichment of the lives of individual men, women, and children. This power to pass judgment on the worth of the institutions under which they live is both a moral and a legal right of the citizens of a democratic society.

This social-democratic conception and practice also has implications for our view of morals. On its basis, morals no longer constitute a realm apart from ordinary social experience. The field of morals is continuous with the whole field of human relationships. The human effect of each established community practice is a concern of morals thus conceived. In order to be intelligent about moral questions, we must be intelligent about the concrete affairs of economy, technology, science, government, family, and international life—about all the constituents that enter into consequences and accordingly into the determination of policies. As new ways of living are institutionalized, as new schedules of individual rights and obligations are developed, the morality of a group undergoes change, because morality means finding and doing the best that is possible. Hence social democracy maintains that all, not a special class, should share in the conservation and the elaboration of the morality of a people. It likewise denies that morality can be given a more secure foundation than that which the processes of experience provide. It is the faith of a social democracy that from within the context of shared experience, by the reflective evaluation of both means and consequences, all necessary moral ideals and standards can be developed. Democracy therefore calls for a society in which there will be full and free interaction of group with group, in order that decisions about the common ways of life may be informed with real appreciation of the bearing these institutionalized practices have on the life of all members of the community.

Thus the implications of both political and social democracy point to the need for a particular kind of school. They require that the school be so designed and conducted that its activities within and outside of the classroom will illustrate basic respect for each and every human personality. They also require a school in which the young will have opportunity to mingle with all elements of their community, and hence come to know and to have a regard for individuals from different social, racial, religious, and occupational groups. Above all, they require a school in which the young will become acquainted with the moral and spiritual heritage of the race that they may become more wise in dealing with the institutions and life conditions of their society.

RELIGION AND SECULAR EDUCATION

From the beginning of the Republic, many of our leaders have realized that American democracy requires a distinctive school. They have urged a kind of education which would cherish as its supreme purposes the nurture of the sense of community in the young and the enlightenment of both children and parents. These leaders knew that democracy is a worthy but exacting way of life and that its essential practices, attitudes, and allegiances are not biologically transmitted and therefore do not spontaneously unfold within the experience of the young.

Through the provision of a common system of free schools, supported and controlled by the whole civil community and hence free from sectarian bias, the American people sought to meet these crucial educational needs of their society. Devoted as they were to spiritual ideals, they were nevertheless gradually led by stubborn experience to develop a secular system of public education. This educational action did not signify any indifference on their part to the ethical values of the Western religious tradition. On the contrary, the American people in developing more consistently the implications of democracy for civic and educational affairs were making a creative extension of these historical, religious insights. In this evolving democratic pattern, respect for human personality is now broadened to mean not only accepting the individual as the supreme object of moral consideration but also making him a full and equal partner in the development of the community, including the further molding of its basic patterns of economy, government, and morality.

The democratic American community was unwilling to exclude any individual, or group, from this common social undertaking because of religious factors. It was felt that although classical religion had been influenced by deep-moving tendencies of the age, it had not, as yet, undertaken those reconstructions in many of its branches which would make it possible for it to operate without disruptive civil conflict. Its sectarian divisions, methods, and interpretations did not harmonize with the non-parochial patterns of freedom of thought, experimental science, and the kind of community co-operation essential to social and political democracy. Hence respect for individual human personality, which is the heart of the democratic ethic, required that religion, at least in its present stage of development, be made a private not a public affair.

It apparently was also recognized that until the history, the theologies, the institutions, and the rites of religion can be studied by the same objective, empirical methods—anthropological, comparative, historical, and experimental—which are used in the treatment of other subject matters of human experience, the public school would have to be on its guard against any and all proposals to make religion an organic part of the curriculum. Already in the literature, fine arts, history, and social science courses, and in the observance of religious and national holidays and the like, religion now receives, with public approval, a considerable attention in the work of the public school. As we have also emphasized, the public school is wholeheartedly committed to the democratic way of life with all that implies for the cultivation of ethical outlooks and spiritual values in the emotional and intellectual dispositions of the young.

Whenever and wherever the leaders and adherents of the various churches agree that the creeds and the rival claims and practices of religion can be studied by the ordinary, empirical procedures characteristic of the other work of the public school, little difficulty will be experienced in making a study of these aspects of religion also a part of the program of public education. Until that more ideal situation is reached in the religious life of the country, the present working arrangement is likely to be continued.

Certainly, the spiritual life of American democracy will not be enriched, but impoverished, if the public schools are compelled to give up their allegiance to freedom of thought and to the scholarly study of whatever subjects they are asked to bring within the range of the experience of the young. It is also doubtful if the interests of a truly spiritual religion would, in the long run, be advanced were it to come to rely on an authoritarian use of the coercive powers of the secular state for its own development.

Chapter V

SPIRITUAL VALUES AND PUBLIC AND RELIGIOUS EDUCATION

EDUCATION AND THE QUEST FOR HAPPINESS

MAN'S restless quest for happiness and the part in this quest served by the American public school are the concern of this book. Education appears in the light of something more than learning the fundamentals of adjusting to the social and physical environment, and of assuring vocational success. It becomes considerably more than an instrument by which bloodless and abstract aims are to be attained. Rather, it is regarded as the core of the surging experience of childhood and youth through which the person develops ideals of what he would be and what he would do, and through experiment, study, and co-operative living acquires the abilities that aid him in some measure to realize these ideals. The realization is always incomplete and imperfect, yet as long as new ideals emerge from experience and the person steadfastly and prudently pursues them, gaining increase in skill and knowledge, and appreciation for his course of life as a search for something beyond him, he is growing in happiness.

It is this search for what is good that distinguishes man from other animals,—this, and his ability to evaluate what is good or better when it is found, and his genius for seeing, in any good experience, the possibilities for greater good beyond. Further, man differentiates the good he seeks into the good of beauty, the good of truth, and the good of ethical conduct. The questing, and the ability in some measure to clarify and evaluate the object of the quest, combine to form the dynamic principle of human experience. As experience develops in accordance with this principle, there is an accompanying feeling of happy fulfillment; to the extent that experience is blocked, diverted, or distorted, there is misery. The principle sounds abstract, and like all principles, it is. But applied to life itself, the seeking of love and friendship, of the beautiful in music and poetry, the truth in science and literature, and justice in the relationship between men in society, it takes on the color and warmth of life and reveals its significance.

Those objects of man's concern have value in the spiritual sense which when pursued give a greater sense of happiness. The desire for gain alone is not spiritual, because gain does not bring happiness; yet if this desire is secondary in the course of building up a business, or a professional practice, or in doing a craftsmanlike job, it can accompany an activity definitely filled with spiritual value, and itself acquire spiritual significance. The desire for sex gratification alone is not spiritual, but sexual expression in genuine loves does have such value. Spiritual value is the value placed on ideals and the experiential process of approximating ideals. Those ideals are valued more (are higher) which have a richer and more complex content.

Clearly, then, education carried on properly in the public school should contribute immensely to the child's pursuit of happiness. For it presents a controlled environment in which guided experience takes its course; out of it grow ideas; as value is placed on these ideas, they become ideals—what the child wants to know, to do, and to be, as well as guides for knowing, doing, and becoming. The greater the content of these ideals (the greater relation there is between aspiration, knowledge, skill, imagery, and sensation), the greater pleasure is experienced in their realization. Growth in experience is the actualization of the potentialities of experience; it is the teacher's function to recognize the potentialities and to provide the richest and most stimulating setting possible.

NATURAL RATHER THAN SUPERNATURAL VALUES AS THE CONCERN OF THE SCHOOL

An objection may arise to the position taken by this book and it may be stated as follows: Spiritual values are supernatural, and since the public school is not concerned with religion, it should not be concerned with such values. Spiritual values are not, however, exclusively supernatural, any more than spiritual virtues (certain good habits upon which high value is placed) are exclusively so. A distinction is generally made between the supernatural and the natural virtues. The supernatural virtues are FAITH (knowledge of God), HOPE (desire of God), and CHARITY (love of God). The major natural virtues are TEMPERANCE, JUSTICE, and FORTITUDE (called moral virtues), and INTELLIGENCE, KNOWLEDGE, and WISDOM (intellectual virtues); PRUDENCE is regarded as both an intellectual and a moral virtue. The natural virtues are acquired through natural experience, although the church teaches that their development may be aided supernaturally. The fact is that in so far as the public school educator can and does strive to bring out the spiritual values implicit in natural experience, he does not do so in competition with the church.

The public school is the agent of the family and of society as it is organized in the state. The family can no longer carry on the educative function alone, because of the increasing complexity of civilized life. Hence a large part of it has been delegated to the school, which has been provided by the state in the interest of the common good. It does not, therefore, compete with the church. In fact, the public school has been completely secularized to eliminate any such competition. The school is not "Godless," but restricted so far as the teaching of religion is concern so that the religious rights and prerogatives of citizens will not be infringed upon by the school any more than by any other agency of the state. By shaping education so that experiences of high spiritual value receive greater emphasis, the public school is not usurping the function of the church.

By the same token, the public school is not in competition with parochial schools in any other realm of experience than the natural. In the realm of natural experience, it competes with the parochial school as it does with any other private school. It is argued that a single public school system has a decided advantage over a multiple system of public, private, and parochial schools on the following grounds: If all children are brought together for a large part of the time, those differences which cause misunderstanding, religious and economic differences, will not loom so large, nor will they become focal points from which hostile attitudes spread. When one minority withdraws its children from schools on the basis of religion, and another on the basis of social-economic status, both of them are likely to be misunderstood by the majority. And in time of crisis, the misunderstanding may have serious results. Free choice in such matters must be guaranteed; yet every effort should be made by the public school and those who support it to gain and merit the confidence of those who would withdraw their children from it, and to persuade them not to do so if national and local community of spirit is to be achieved.

Conditions have existed that undermined the confidence of many people in the public schools, particularly in large cities. The school population is heterogeneous, and the support of the school has been about at the subsistence level. Parents are much concerned, naturally, for the moral and social welfare of their children, and several courses are open to those who can afford it. They may move to a "better" neighborhood or community where their children will associate with a much more homogeneous group of children, and where better instructional facilities are available in the community school. They may send their children to a private school where there will be a "better class" of children, or to a parochial school where religious and moral instruction is provided to a group of children who have a common religion. It is all very well to speak to parents of the broader social contacts the child will make in the public school, and to tell them that such broad contacts will make for social unity and democracy. It is the very broadness of the contacts that frightens them, for they would not have their children, if they can help it, exposed to an environment where unpleasant and socially undesirable characteristics at the least, and positively immoral behavior at the worst, may be acquired. It is not always indefensible snobbery that leads parents to an undemocratic decision; most frequently it is fear.

Private and parochial schools were established at a time when there were no adequate public schools, and their continuance is a criticism of the public school; as the public schools improve, however, the need of private and church enterprise in education will diminish. The public school will succeed in becoming the school for all the people under the following circumstances: when a rich, full program is possible because the school is adequately supported; when teachers are not so burdened with large classes and administrative duties that they make each child a minute element in the pattern of their routine; when teachers are chosen not only on the basis of their training but also on the basis of a personality that will have an uplifting effect upon children, and because they have a true vocation, that is, because they have genuine affection for children and a love of teaching.

Progress is being made in these directions now. The public school is being conducted more and more in such a fashion that the essential virtues are developed in all children, even those who come from morally poor homes and neighborhoods. The program of slum clearance and the elimination of social conditions that breed vice are aiding the school immensely in its task of unifying the community. Not only as the schools are better supported, but as the population becomes more homogeneous through improved living conditions for all the people and the elimination of squalor, will the ideal be approximated. Furthermore, as spiritual values receive more and more emphasis in the school, and it regards its purposes as larger than teaching mere literacy and the fundamental intellectual operations, it will contribute to the greater harmony as well as the greater happiness of the people. In the meantime, public and non-public (private and parochial) schools exist side by side, and since all are concerned with the development of full persons and good citizens, there is and should be no conflict between them.

Is there any danger that the public school will teach secularism, or the denial of religion? In so far as the public school does not concern itself with religion, would that be sufficient reason for opposition to its growth on the part of those definitely interested in religion? The reason for keeping religion out of the school has already been mentioned. If it were taught, who would teach it as a part of the regular program? No one would be happy if religion were taught unless he was assured that the teacher was of his own religious persuasion. It has been suggested by some that religions might be presented objectively and dispassionately to school children as a part of general culture. But if the entire emotional content of religion were drained off so that it was not religion at all that was being taught, skepticism would result. This would place the schools in the hands of the agnostics and atheists. The presentation of religion to all children in a school where there is a heterogeneity of religious belief, then, could take two courses: either open proselytizing for a particular belief or open proselytizing for atheism. Either course would split the community wide open and in the process perpetrate a horrible injustice.

Many public schools are providing released time for religious instruction which may be offered within the school building by authorized representatives of the churches involved. This has the advantage of keeping all children under the same roof and making all their school experience common except that part devoted to religious instruction. If communities and churches will co-operate in this use of the public school, the school will advance measurably in gaining the confidence and full support of all elements in the community, and children will not be divided into groups which may regard each other with mutual suspicion and even hostility when they are called upon to work together in later life.

THE CHURCH, THE STATE, AND THE PUBLIC SCHOOL

Because the school is public and state controlled, is it likely to advocate some form of statism, the superiority of the state to the individual person, and in so doing come into conflict with the churches? In other words, must the church itself educate in order to protect man from subjection to a monstrous state?

There is no real danger of the American public school's teaching any form of statism. It teaches the processes of government in a democratic state, but it teaches that the best form of government known to man, the democratic form, is a means to man's development and not an end in itself. The state, however, is a necessary means to such development, for it is inconceivable that proper development of the individual occur outside of the community of the state, which is a formal organization of individual persons based on organic law and statute, designed to insure the common good, the good of its members. It is a means to the fulfillment of all the potentialities for growth with which its constituents are endowed, and certainly not an organization that transcends the person, or that is contrary to his best interests. It protects the citizen from injustice and stays him from committing unjust acts against others, thereby making him a better man.

The state has authority over the citizen and demands obedience from him, for its laws embody the principles of justice resulting from man's inquiry and experience over a period of centuries. Plato provides an interesting statement on the relation of the individual to the state in the *Crito*. Socrates in prison has listened patiently to Crito's offer to help him escape, and his justification of the offer on the grounds that the sentence was unjust. In Socrates' answer, the following is found:

> And when we (the citizens) are punished by her (the state), whether with imprisonment or stripes, the punishment is to be endured in silence; and if she lead us to wounds or death in battle, thither we must follow, as is right; neither may anyone yield or retreat or leave his rank, but whether in battle or in court of law, or in any other place, he must do what his city and his country order him; or he must change their view of what is just.[1]

The democratic principle resides in the last clause: "or he must change their view of what is just." Obedience to the state and defense of its integrity is demanded not because the state is the master of the person, but because it is the only means of guarantee that the person may realize himself. It is a necessary means, a *finis quo*, as St. Thomas calls it, an *end by which* man fulfills his destiny. Good citizenship is the prime requisite for self-realization, and there is always the recourse of changing the laws to secure greater justice. Because of what the state does for the person, it can exercise certain rights over him in return.

The school, in building a common culture, teaches loyalty to the state that maintains the common good, and teaches the responsibility of the state for protecting its citizens in the exercise of their rights and privileges, among which is the right to worship in any church, or to assemble in any group for any purpose which does not threaten injustice to other citizens of the state or the impairment of the common good.

The church, while not subject to the state, aids it tremendously. For example, the Roman Catholic Church has proved

---

[1] Benjamin Jowett, translator, *The Dialogues of Plato* (New York: The Macmillan Company), Vol. II, pp. 152-153.

a most effective factor in the Americanization of immigrants from the middle of the last century onward. In the church, the poor and ignorant Catholics from oppressed lands found one familiar institution in the strange new country, something they understood and could depend upon. It built and supported schools for those who otherwise would have been neglected. Through these schools families were held together, for they were taught by nuns from the same class and countries as the parents of the children in the parish. The child, therefore, felt no shame or guilt because his parents came from a country and a people despised by the teacher, and he saw nothing to despise in his parents because they differed from the native citizens. The teaching itself was a work of love and devotion carried on by women whose only worldly interest was their work, and whose only objects of worldly affection were the children in their parish. American ways and institutions were explained to foreigners whose lot was poverty and exploitation at the hands of those who had been in the country longer than they.

The success of the Bishops in quelling the draft riots during the Civil War shows forcibly how one serious problem, brought about by the ignorance of the immigrants and the neglect and greed of native citizens was met by the Church in the interest of the welfare of the state. The task of building public schools to their present size would have been much more difficult, and expensive, had there not been so many parochial schools already in existence. It would have been even a longer time before schools for all the people had been established, and those who needed the schools most, the children of immigrants, would have become a much greater problem. The church has not been so active in establishing new elementary schools recently, because the great influx is now over, and masses of Catholics are not being imported to work in the mines and the mills. Yet the established schools, in the absence of adequate public school facilities, are still performing their function of assimilation in large industrial centers. Additions to the Catholic educational system more recently have been at the higher levels, where public education has not expanded sufficiently to meet the need, and private education is economically (in the great colleges) and religiously (in the small denominational colleges) discriminatory.

THE CURRICULUM AND NATURAL VALUES OF THE SPIRIT

The natural experiences children have in the school should have a high spiritual value in so far as they should give the child the feeling of exaltation and gratification that accompanies growth in control of his environment and of his own powers through proper direction of his activities. The adjective "worth while" is applied to these activities because they are interesting in themselves rather than leading as means to some end psychologically far removed. In other words, they are completely absorbing, permitting the release of controlled and directed energies in their course.

The child engaged in arithmetic is not merely learning something that will be useful to him. He is developing a mastery over abstract relationships that man alone among the animals can master. This mastery affords him an immense satisfaction while he is acquiring it, and his pleasure increases as his mastery increases. The pleasure of mastery, its *value* to the child, is not likely to be achieved if only its usefulness is stressed—its usefulness in later life, its usefulness in gaining the praise of teacher or parent, or in avoiding their displeasure. It can be achieved if the development, the fulfillment of the child's nature in a process of marshalling abstract concepts and relationships becomes more and more explicit as the aim of instruction. It is not unlike the pleasure accruing from the process of playing games in which certain objectives are set up and achieved in the face of competition. The exaltation that comes from the successful co-ordination of the body and its exercise in accordance with the rules of the game is a spiritual matter. Games are useful for the physical development of a body that must be strong and flexible to meet the rigors of life, but again, the usefulness is an incidental value. The prime value of the game is the spiritual lift it affords through the liberation of powers, and its secondary value is the feeling of physical well-being that ensues.

In recent years there has been an increased emphasis upon "creative expression" through the media of the graphic arts, manual arts, music, and written as well as oral expression. The school has made considerable progress in devising methods and procedures for children to express themselves through these media. Some attempts have been more successful than others, but the most successful have been those in which expression has been carefully guided to the primary end of the child's realizing the desire to express himself through a mastery of the media in which he was called upon to work. Those attempts have been relatively unsuccessful where free expression was not consistently guided to mastery, or where the freedom of expression was only a motivating device by which the child was induced to undertake an activity in which he felt no real purpose.

The social studies in the school curriculum give the child an insight into, and an appreciation of, the different communities of which he is a member—the family, the local community, the nation, and the world. They recognize that the fulfillment of the child's nature does not take place in a social environment that is abstract, but in a warm, living matrix that nourishes his growth through a multiplicity of sub-organizations. All of this must be made explicit through the social studies curriculum.

In the earliest grades, and with somewhat decreasing emphasis as the child matures, the family is the center of concern. It is the simplest community, and the one in which he enjoys the most intimate of social contacts—the love of parents, brothers, and sisters. In it he finds security and worth; he learns pride and loyalty; he is subject to authority and discipline, and acquires the beginnings of the social virtues that will later expand and become more ramifying in their implications as his social circle increases. The school supplements and strengthens the attitudes developed in the home, guides their spread to the wider relationships of the child as he matures. To the extent that the school succeeds, the child finds himself "at home," and happy in larger and larger groups.

His very enrollment in the school introduces him to a community of children and adults, and it is there he learns the history, geography, and economic organization of the community in which he resides, whether it is an urban or a rural one. His desire to seek satisfaction in relation to other children is recognized, and he is helped to join natural groupings in and out of school. As he studies the interrelatedness of the elements of his local community, he acquires an understanding similar to that he has of his family. He learns the functions of its institutions, he learns the organization of authority—what privileges he has and what his duties are. He learns landmarks, and associates them with characters and events in local history. He discovers that the community, like the family, is a natural organization in which he can realize his powers, that its other members are warm, with ambitions and affections like his own, that it offers, not only a milieu for action, but security and refuge, and deserves his loyalty and help. It is his, and he becomes proud of it, and comforted by the friends he finds in it. Without it, he would not only be less than a man, he could not live.

The state is a larger, more inclusive community than either the family or the local community, and it is more perfect because it is more self-sufficient. It underwrites the privileges one has in the family and town; it assures the exercise of rights and protects citizens from external aggressors as well as from injustice within the state. Although more removed from the individual, as he develops he recognizes it for what it is—not only a benefactor but something to be proud of. He comes to love the fatherland and its institutions. He reveres the national heroes and his emotions rise as he contemplates their fortitude and the courage of the anonymous millions who have made it what it has become. He throws himself into the study of how it can progress in the administration of justice, and in such improvement of its institutions as will assure greater freedom for the development of all of its citizens. The nation has its rituals, those attendant upon the flag, the re-enactment of historical events, displays of national unity, and military parades. The growing person, attending these rituals and becoming acquainted with the history of the nation, comes more and more to value the nation that, through its laws, stimulates the growth of virtue in him and does so much to make him a complete man.

The child, then, begins and pursues his development in a family where he enjoys the love of parents, brothers, and sisters. As he gets older and establishes his own family, he still relies on the intimate affection of his brothers and sisters and their families. He is, as a child and a man, a member of groups, clubs, fraternities, and service clubs. He is a respected citizen of a town, a voter, probably allied with a political party, and a citizen of the state. In these multiple organizations, he experiences affection, friendship, respect, or the feeling of personal worth, and justifiable pride. He learns from his associations the virtues of courage, temperance, justice, and prudence, none of which could be acquired without the stimulus afforded by particular social pressure, but which, in acquisition, are self-satisfying and lead to happiness. The public school is a most important agent in bringing about and guiding this development from the immediate, intimate relationships of the family to more expansive relationships in the community and in the nation.

The arts (literature, music, and the other fine arts) reveal the beauty in human experience—the beauty (which Plato identifies with the abstract good) that is the goal of man's restless, searching spirit. Great works of art intensify experience, make clear universal principles of experience, and give experience unity. They are landmarks in man's triumph over chaotic bewilderment, and the confusion of values that characterizes his immediate, untutored vision of the universe in which he finds himself. In the past, the common school has only been interested in the fundamentals of literacy. Niggardly support, the predominantly puritanical suspicion that the arts were Romish, or the indulgence of ne'er-do-wells, and the artistically impoverished background of teachers have all militated against the flourishing of the arts in the school. However, they are rapidly coming into their own; unappreciative analysis, vapid "enjoyment," and pointless "self-expression" are giving way to a well-ordered introduction to the arts as those means through which men's vision of the beauty and truth they constantly seek in experience is realized.

Experience is intensified by the literary artist who, in a play or novel, selects characters with whom the reader identifies himself, and places them in a setting of experience that the reader can understand. The conflict between good and evil, the conflict of motives—wealth, fame, love, and duty—and the conflict between the appetites and reason are presented more intensely than in everyday experience. In response to one character, a tragic one, the reader may say, "There, but for the grace of God, go I"; in another character he sees how man triumphs over frustration of the spirit by fate, by men, and by institutions; in still another, a comic character, he sees the ludicrousness of human convention, ignorance, or vanity. He recognizes, to an intensified degree, the confusion and indecision attendant upon making choices in a difficult universe of experience. The art product is absorbing to the extent that the reader identifies himself with the course of experience portrayed; it delights to the extent that he recognizes the realization of human potentialities that reside in human nature. The painter sees with a clearer eye what all men want to see, yet of which they are but indistinctly aware in the course of ordinary experience, and the hearing of the musician is more sensitive to the tones that all wish to hear.

In the vision of the artist, experience is not only intensified; its principles become more clear, and unity is achieved. Universal ideas are particularized in the work of art and blossom into meaning. The classics are timeless because they embody principles governing human behavior at all times and under all circumstances. They show how the human spirit aspires to the good, and how, through vices of excess or defect, they miss their goals. They show above all, however, that life itself is a work of art, an achievement, and by sharpening the senses and understanding of the reader help him to "be of one piece," to orient and integrate his activities, to find more pleasure and therefore more meaning in his own immediate experience; in brief, they help him to clarify his own ideals and to enjoy fully the process of moving toward their realization. Of all the arts, music is generally regarded as the most absorbing; it affords perfect release for the energies of the senses and the spirit. It is a most hopeful sign that musical performance, instrumental and vocal, is being stressed more and more in the school, since appreciation of music increases as skill is acquired in creating it. The dreadful drum and bugle corps which sprang up in schools throughout the country bore testimony to the fact that children want to play, and could be taught in the schools. They have given a strong impetus to the teaching of genuine music.

THE NEW EMPHASIS IN THE PUBLIC SCHOOL

The activities provided in the school curriculum and in the general living together within the whole life of the school build up in the child an appreciation of the spiritual values in natural living. Because activities are selected which are the most direct means to the ends of growth, and progress in growth is guided and controlled, the experience of growth is intensified over what it would be were the child left to himself. He sees himself getting somewhere. By the same token, ideals become clarified; the child is able to see and define his goals more clearly, even though the definition is far from perfect. The beginnings of integrity of purpose therefore may be learned, and the organization of means and ends will improve as the adult continues through life. Under these circumstances, the powers of the person develop harmoniously, and because the goal is development, and not the acquisition of heterogeneous and opposed material goods, a happy growth is assured.

The church traditionally provided a haven for the great masses of civilized people, for it was there pre-eminently that spiritual fulfillment could be realized. It guaranteed the dignity of the person and it preached the satisfaction of a heavenly kind that would come through good works and faith. It assured love to those who did not have it. It assured a place in heaven to those who had none on earth. It confirmed the promise of position in the community of saints to those without position in the earthly community. The supernatural goals of religion made life livable for many men and women throughout the ages. Religion has been somewhat neglected in America because men could rise, under frontier conditions. It was believed that money, position, and fame could be had by those born in impoverished circumstances; the high standard of living gave renewed promise, even to those who failed. A cult of success, of material success, arose, and people struggled for the prosperity that was "just around the corner" until they were saddened and burdened with the futility of the struggle.

This narrowly materialistic view is now breaking down because it has proved and must prove both unethical and impractical. Material success is a frustrating goal, frustrating to the spirit because it can never be achieved. People feel that they are underestimated, underpaid, that they do not amount to much by material standards. They constantly fear the imminence of failure according to these standards, or feel that judged by them they have already failed. This is the expected and normal outcome of any system that entertains strictly materialistic goals. There is no satisfaction in them because they cannot, in any ultimate sense, be achieved. They are always competitive. One who succeeds in amassing wealth compares what he has amassed with the wealth of others; he who succeeds in rising in the social scale compares himself unfavorably with others who have risen higher.

The school is shifting its emphasis to attain a clearer focus on its problem. Educational psychology has been abstract. In the attempt to make learning and development understandable, materialistic explanations for human phenomena have been presented, and they have led educators, in theory at least, to discount the spiritual nature of man—many texts in educational psychology have gone out of the way to ridicule any but mechanical descriptions of human behavior. The gap between educational theory and practice can pretty much be accounted for here. The practical art of education has been in the hands of warmhearted teachers whose affection for students has given them intuitive insight into their need for satisfaction. The problem with which they are consistently confronted has been the translation of cold, abstract principles into the warm, living milieu in which the child grows.

The finest essence of the progressive education movement, however, has done much to bring about the adjustment of verifiable abstract principles to the full living of the child in the classroom. Its methods fuse the resources of science and the teacher's personality in the approach to child experience. It advocates and practices the method of concrete, full experience, not only because scientifically learning is most effective through this approach, but also because of the satisfaction the child feels, the self-fulfillment he experiences. Religion is not involved in any of these activities. Progressive education is sometimes called "naturalistic," but it should preferably be called "natural." "Naturalism" is a doctrine that natural principles, discovered by inquiry as opposed to revelation, provide the only source of truth. Whereas "naturalism" is opposed to supernatural religion, and denies it, "natural education" limits itself to the natural sphere, but does not categorically deny or oppose education based on religious sources and leading to supernatural goals.

THE SECULARIST ERROR

The question still arises: Can spiritual values be taught in a secular setting? Assume there is no conflict between church and state in education, can those people who adhere to no church and no religious education provide for their children as full a development as those who supplement public education with religious education? There is disagreement on this matter. Some argue that man's real spiritual life is in the natural community in which he finds himself, and that the spiritual virtues are best developed in such a community (see Chapter II). It is further argued that religious education spreads authoritarian control and diminishes the freedom of the individual person to frame and fulfill purposes in the light of his own intelligence. This argument is embedded in the secularist point of view as presented in the preceding chapter.

It is argued by those who believe religious education has an important place that the very factors making the natural community valuable for the development of the individual person are found to a more expansive and permeating degree in the larger supernatural and timeless community of the Hebraic-Christian church, and that the secularist position is a narrow and abstract one. The social virtues indeed have spiritual values; progress in social understanding, tolerance, co-operation and respect for the personality of others, even though their opinions show that they are the result of primitive thinking, are much to be desired. But a program that consciously excludes religious development of the person is not concerned with the whole person any more than a program that consciously excludes his aesthetic development would be. Religion constitutes man's seeking for a good that is more comprehensive than the social good. The social good is only part of it, and violence is done to human nature if the social good is made the chief good, and the search for it and devotion to it is substituted for religion. Those who hold this view feel that whereas religion should not be compulsory in the public school curriculum, religious education is of vital importance for the development of the person and should be encouraged by means that do no injustice to others not of the same mind.

Advocates of complete secularism in education believe that religious institutions have an authoritarian tradition adversely affecting the freedom of personal development. Authoritarianism, the exclusive reliance upon the authority of the state or the church in all matters, even those pertaining to private thought and inquiry that should be a matter of indifference to these two institutions, is a phenomenon of tyranny in the state and of clericalism in the church. Tyranny needs no definition, but clericalism does. When the clergy becomes so powerful that it is a privileged class (as it was in France before the French Revolution, for example) in its pride, it crushes the individual, using its knowledge and position to further itself at the expense of the common good. It can also employ, as it did, its prestige as the guardian of religion to further its own material interests. This is an evil recognized and deplored by the church, and strongly guarded against. There is no such power in the clergy today, and the perfect separation of church and state provided by the United States Constitution makes it unlikely that clericalism can ever arise in this country. The clergy has no influence over the people save in matters of morals and supernatural faith.

Secularists also seem to hold that any body of belief which cannot be publicly and objectively verified by human intelligence with the aid of human instruments is suspect, and that revealed religion is such a suspect body of belief. They reason next that all knowledge based on revelation has a basis that must not be questioned, and therefore has behind it the force of authority and not the logic of human reason. The next inference seems to be that this authority somehow stems through the attitude of all people who have declared their faith in the supernatural and that their reasoning in the natural sphere is based, to some extent, at least, upon authoritarian principles. The fallacy here lies in the fact that the conclusion does not follow from the premises. If it were granted that revealed religion is not subject to question (and the entire history of Christianity contradicts this premise) and that theology is based upon unquestioned supernatural principles, it would not follow that in the sphere of natural action, moral or intellectual, reason is overruled by authority. If authoritarianism means, as it does strictly, that authority is the only basis, the exclusive basis of knowledge and control of conduct, then there is no such thing in the church, save in the negligibly small fanatical sects. The church holds man to be rational and to possess free will, and has not ever denied the right to make a choice based on personal rational deliberation.

It does, however, offer guidance. It supports the substitutive authority of the teacher (the authority over those who do not know right from wrong until they mature) and the essential authority of the state (the natural authority that must reside in state officials if certain actions for the common good are to be pursued). The danger of secularism, if the movement attains any strength, is that in the interest of freedom from religion it will deprive men of their right of freedom of worship.

Freedom in democracy means freedom of the individual person within limits. One is not free to commit unjust acts against his neighbors. He is not free to act imprudently to the detriment of his neighbors or his family (compulsory school laws protect children against such parental imprudence). One is not free to be intemperate to the extent that he is a public nuisance, nor to lack knowledge of what he can do and what he must do, and what is forbidden him (his rights and duties) as a citizen. He is free to develop as a person, and this development is guided and bounded by the experience of men as a whole as to what is best. Freedom of thought does not mean freedom to think wrongly on matters that are of considerable consequence to the general welfare.

Dewey has taken the stand that freedom means freedom of intelligence, the liberation of purpose. His is a program of education in the knowledges and skills necessary to overcome, in the fulfillment of purpose, obstacles in the physical environment and maladjustments in the social environment which may be attributed to men's lacking the knowledge and insight for getting on well in a community life which is becoming more and more complex. Study and experimentation are necessary for this. The opposition is ignorance in general, and not a chimera of authoritarianism. The church does not oppose experimentation or new ideas so long as they are not occasions of viciousness. A harmful practice or an irrational idea cannot be made good or rational simply by tagging it as liberal or democratic. It must stand the test of deliberation and objective test, if the latter is still necessary, before it is accepted. By the same token, a rational belief should not be rejected because it has been tagged authoritarian.

CONCLUSION

Spiritual development, it seems, can be brought about through the public school system as it liberates children from ignorance and makes it possible for them to pursue their purposes, and as it helps them to acquire the virtues of courage, temperance, justice, and prudence in the pursuit. These are natural virtues and result in natural happiness. The public school has no quarrel with religious schools or with those people who wish their children to acquire an education in the supernatural virtues for a world beyond this one. It does seem unwise for a separate school system to be established because that would lead to divisiveness in the community and mutual bigotry. Misunderstanding between groups in any community is usually due to ignorance, to the lack of familiarity with the other elements. To bring children up in completely different schools may weaken, because of ignorant persecution, the position of the minority group, and by so doing, weaken the community as a whole. There is no individual freedom in any community where there is danger of dissension; for there is no trust.

Chapter VI

LEARNING SPIRITUAL VALUES

FROM one point of view it would have been more logical to write this chapter title as "Teaching Spiritual Values." But the verb *to teach* so often carries an authoritarian halo that it seems better to treat the learning process first and then, on the basis thus laid, discuss the matter of teaching. Some readers may at first question the extended presentation of certain fairly familiar details of the learning process, but the treatment adopted seems necessary in order to lay an adequate foundation for the later discussions.

THE PSYCHOLOGY OF LEARNING

Learning in Relation to Living. Many people, when the question of learning is raised, think first of school, of assigned lessons, of learning these lessons out of books, of reciting then to teachers, of learning today what can be put to use only later—possibly only when one is grown. A different conception of learning is here held. We may by contrast call it life's learning, though it should rule in school as well. In this, what is learned is learned as and because it is lived, here and now. And the learning, we may say, is practically automatic and inevitable; the actual living itself effects the learning, more or less strongly. And the more strongly the thing is lived, the more strongly it is learned.

How these things are so we shall see in the following discussion; but they are not to be thought of as new or uncertain or not yet established. On the contrary, Plato took the same position in Theaetetus (176f.) when he told how the penalty of wrongdoing is not external punishment, "which evil doers often escape," but "a penalty which cannot be escaped," namely, that the person by reason of his evil deeds inherently grows evil. Emerson saw and said the same thing only positively: "He who does a good deed is instantly ennobled." In other words, we learn what we live, we become what we choose in our own hearts as our ways of behaving. It is in this same way that our youth must learn the spiritual values of our civilization, values first sensed by the supreme spiritual masters of the world in their deepest moments and shown to the rest of us as the best available ways of living yet discovered among men. Our youth must live these values in their natural setting of use if they are to learn them.

That brilliant young Britisher, W. K. Clifford (1845-1879), gives in his oft-quoted words a good introduction to our discussion: "It is the peculiarity of living things not merely that they change [that is, behave] under the influence of surrounding circumstances, but that any change [behavior] which takes place in them is not lost, but retained and, as it were, built into the organism to serve as a foundation for future action."[1]

We use the verb *to learn* for describing this peculiarity of living things. It means the acquiring of new ways of behaving. Learning these so changes a person as to modify his further behavior. "Learning is any activity that produces a relatively permanent effect on later activity."[2]

We wish here to note how intimately learning is bound up with living and how the two interact. We may begin with adult learning; though children and youth learn on substantially these same principles. Clifford means us to see that living inherently carries learning along with it—we auto-

[1] *Lectures and Essays* (New York: Truth Seeker Company, 1886), Vol. I, p. 88.

[2] R. S. Woodworth, *Psychology* (New York: Henry Holt & Company, 1940), 4th ed., p. 292.

matically and inevitably learn what we live[3]—and the living so stored up in learning "serves as a foundation for future action." Thus it is that past experience remains with us to guide and give content to future experience. In this sense, learning is like all other organic behavior. It grows out of the present experience but looks to the future. A friend invites me to a golf game; we discuss it. I accept. Here a brief experience, limited in time to a telephone conversation, puts into my stream of life among other things a proposal considered and a decision made. The proposal as accepted stays with me during the intervening days and guides my pertinent further steps until I enter the actual golf game. What I lived during the telephoning was fixed for my future by the way I accepted it to act on. A proposal came to my mind, I accepted it in a certain way; as I accepted it, so it stayed with me to re-enter appropriately to help determine my further behavior. This is what learning is and how it serves. In my more conscious living, possible ways of reacting come forward (rise in my mind) for more or less critical consideration; at other times I simply "sense" what to do. In either case what I accept to act on stays with me (as long as it is so accepted) to enter pertinently into my future living. What I originally so live is learned *as* I accept it.

Lest any think this telephone-golf experience too trivial to furnish a foundation for more serious matters, consider December 7, 1941, in the life of America. We heard of the treacherous attack on Pearl Harbor; we accepted what we heard and so learned that Japan was waging war against us. And, further, we felt in this a challenge; we accepted the challenge and

---

[3] This use of *live* as a transitive verb may not at first carry its full import. A few instances taken from the Oxford English Dictionary will perhaps help to give a fuller grasp of the meaning:

  1542. Not only love but also live the gospel [spelling modernized];
  1650. Words not so much to be read as lived;
  1671. He preached the doctrine and lived the application;
  1770. To live a lie;
  1874. To live poetry, indeed, is always better than to write it.

united to fight. The learning on that day was of the present, but it certainly looked to the future; and our acceptance both of the war as a fact and of the will to fight it out to victory was, so far as the psychology of learning goes, the same as that of the conversation and the golf. Here we learned both the present fact (that the war was on) and the future reference (the will to fight it out). This was as serious and inclusive an instance as the former was minor and ephemeral; but the psychology (for the present discussion) was the same.

To sum up, life is a succession of situations and our responses thereto. A situation presents itself, a proposed reaction thereto (one or more) arises to mind. We consider more or less, and somehow dispose of the proposal. As we accept it (or reject it), so we learn it. As we learn it, so we use it now and also later as occasion may arise (use it as we originally accepted it so long as we continue so to accept it). "What we learn," says Gates, "is a reaction"; "one learns precisely the reaction he hits upon." Guthrie says, "A student does not learn what was in a lecture or in a book. He learns only what the lecture or the book caused him to do." "We learn only what we do" and "We learn errors and bad habits as well as success and good habits."[4] The lecture or the book was a situation to the student; at each moment there arose to him the question of how to respond, what to think, what to accept; his answer to this question—how he accepted what was heard or read and how he felt as he listened and thought—whatever responses he then really (acceptingly) made to the situation as he saw it, whatever he thus really lived, that he learned. We learn the content that we really live.

And such learning is going on during all one's waking life. Whether it be an adult or a child or a dog or an earthworm, each one, it appears, learns at each moment what he accepts on his level as his way of acting or living. We learn what we live.

[4] National Society for the Study of Education, 41st Yearbook, Pt. II, pp. 55, 58, 59.

The Factor of Acceptance in the Learning Process. To say
that we learn what we live is a neat and true summary, but it
needs elucidation to see all that is included. In particular, the
crucial role of *acceptance-to-act-on* needs to be made explicit.
What we learn is not the bare facts objectively existent or
taken simply as such. When you speak, I learn not necessarily
what you actually say but what I take you to say; and in this
we often mis-take what has been said. I learn as and what I
accept. But *my* learning goes beyond my bare acceptance, mistaken or not, of the *fact* as to what you said; I learn *to do* or
not to do what you propose or advise. Two hearers may agree
on the words you use but differ in the way they accept the
principle your words would uphold. One accepts your principle as an addition to his philosophy of life; the other rejects
your principle. Each one learns what he lives, each learns your
principle *as* he accepts it, the one to follow it, the other to
reject it. The way it is accepted *to act on* is the crucial factor to
determine the learning and this both as to fact and as to future
conduct.

On September 1, 1939, Germany wantonly attacked Poland.
On that day Great Britain and the United States heard, objectively we may say, the same radio and cable news, and both
learned as fact what they thus heard; but further, they accepted and so learned two quite different responses to the same
bare facts. Each learned what it accepted to act on, Great
Britain to enter the war on the side of Poland, we to stay out
and wait and hope. *Acceptance-to-act-on* is the crucial factor
to determine what, *for behavior purposes*, has been learned.
We learn always what we live, but we learn it as we accept it
to act on.

But the factor of acceptance goes still further; it determines
the *degree* of learning. Contrast the response of this country
on September 1, 1939, as to degree, with its response on
December 7, 1941. In 1941 we not only accepted the facts to
act on them in a different way from 1939—a different direc-

tion, we may say—but what we accepted we accepted more intensely. The acceptance cut deeper, it changed us more. This time we accepted to act positively and to act vigorously. We learned what we lived both times; we learned each *as* we accepted it to act on and we further learned each *in the degree* that we accepted it. So it is: The stronger the acceptance, the stronger the learning, the more the learning changes us, the more insistently does it stay in the current of life to determine what we shall do. A fuller statement regarding learning would then be: *We learn what we live*, and we learn each response *as* we accept it to act on and we learn it *in the degree* that we accept it.

The full significance of this factor of acceptance will appear clearer when we come to the learning of spiritual values. Shakespeare says, "The quality of mercy is not strained." That is, while the law or other authority may compel outward acts which onlookers might call acts of mercy, the quality of mercy comes not by compulsion. It can come only spontaneously from within as the person, being of that kind, sees a situation which so appeals to him—sees a situation which in fact calls out in him the response of mercy. So it will appear of other spiritual values; the spiritual quality is not strained, it must come as an inherent response to a situation personally felt.

It was stated earlier that the stronger the acceptance, the stronger the learning. We can define strength of learning by saying that one instance of learning is to be counted "stronger" than another if in fact it tends to stay longer with one to affect his further conduct or if it tends more strongly to get back into his experience. It is further true that the "strength of acceptance" often appears under the caption of "felt importance." A variant statement might then be that we learn anything in the degree that we count it important. A second factor to increase strength of learning is relatedness. Other things being equal, one thing is better learned than another according as it is better related, is better understood, or qualitatively better fits in with what we already know. A third factor is repetition. Bare repetition does not bring learning, as Thorndike has shown.[5] The new must be seen and accepted in relation. There seems a "psychological limit" to strength of learning; but until that limit is reached a repetition of the factors that of themselves separately bring learning increases the strength of learning.

Learning and Character Building. That learning builds character follows at once from its definition; but for the better directing of the process of character building the actual process itself needs examination.

By character we mean the more or less abiding aggregate of behavior tendencies, especially and ideally as these tendencies are so interrelated and interwoven as to allow the aggregate to function consciously and intelligently as a unity, as an internally interactive whole. Since learning means a change in behavior tendency, each new item learned adds that much to character. But this addition is actually a reconstruction, not simply a mechanical or numerical addition. Each new item learned is somehow interwoven with what was already there, so that both new and old are mutually affected. The new gets part of its character from the old and the old is in part remade by the new. Each new item learned is a response, a response to the situation as this is then effectively sensed. Being a pertinent response, its character has been adapted pertinently to the situation as sized up. Thus the old clearly affects the new. But the new also affects the old, as follows: This is a case of learning and not simply the use of an old habit; there is therefore something new about it, new to the individual if not to the world. This new means at least that a related change has taken place in the previous thinking and acting of the individual. So the old is changed by the new. In these differ-

[5] *Human Learning* (New York: D. Appleton-Centur Company, 1931), Chapters 1, 2.

ent and reconstructive ways, then, the new and the old mutually affect each other.

Thus learning builds the seamless web that is character. Each new learning is interwoven with its particular connections to the old, and each of these older connections had in its turn already been interwoven also as it was learned with all *its* connections then seen and accepted. John Dewey thus says that "character is the name given to the working interaction of habits"; and he goes on, "Were it not for the continued operation of all habits in every act, no such things as character could exist."[6] Learning then inherently and unavoidably builds character, character of its kind, character according to what is lived as this is accepted to act on.

The foregoing will, if we let it, tell us how to guide the process of character building. The clue is *acting on thinking*. If any youth can be induced to follow with reasonable consistency this process of acting on thinking, we can be reasonably sure of his building a moral character that is intelligently effective. As one continually thinks through what to do, he will accumulate stores of ever more reliable thoughts to use. If in addition he will think consistently on some intelligible pattern—say, on the system of cause and effect—he will so relate his accumulated thoughts to each other and to the facts met in experience as to make his stores the more surely available to recall when he shall need them. If, still further, he will consistently *act* on the best *thinking* he can get, he will build an *effectively* moral character. Our guiding must help youth so to *act on thinking*.

In sum, as we guide youth we must help them to work as consistently as we can on these four principles: (1) act on *thinking*, that is, think before you act, think as fully as you reasonably can and should; (2) think on the basis of cause and effect; (3) *act* on the thinking, act always up to the best that

[6] *Human Nature and Conduct* (New York: Henry Holt & Company, 1922), pp. 38, 40.

thinking can find out; (4) continually judge your thinking by the observed outcomes, so as to profit by your mistakes and thus be the better ready to think next time. In the degree that youth (or anyone) will so think and act and judge, each for himself and truly from within, in like degree can we expect them to build effectively intelligent and moral characters.

TEACHING AS GUIDED LIVING

Teaching exists to foster and promote learning. And the young learn what they live. Hence teaching in order to foster learning must foster living, the kind of living fit to be learned and built into character.

The school must thus understand itself as a place of living, a place where a high quality of living is cultivated, the highest quality we can manage. For the children and youth will build into character whatever their quality of living may be. And, further, since they learn what they live *as* they in their hearts accept it, it is unwise if not impossible for the school to set out a compulsory type or content of living in the hope that the youth will thereby surely learn the desired spiritual values through the outwardly or seemingly higher type of living thus enforced upon them. We are not denying that young children are highly docile (as Piaget has well shown), easily susceptible of strong leading from their elders. But traits thus docilely acquired in childhood need for their perpetuation to be carefully protected from later critical thinking. Such a regime, we think, makes rather for blind obedience and unintelligent conformity than for the creative spiritual quality herein chiefly sought. Nor are we denying a possible emergency use of compulsion. But we cannot hope for continual success from coercion. We cannot, for example, enforce generosity or consideration of others; for too often the youth would fail of inward acceptance of such an enforced regime, fail of hearty acceptance even when actual rebellion did not ensue. And even if youth should accept as docilely as some seem to wish, that would still not suffice for a democratic society. For democracy demands not mere docility but self-reliance, initiative, self-responsibility. And these cannot come by direction from the outside or by compulsion. It would for democracy be a contradiction in terms.

Indeed, when we think of such spiritual matters as appreciating the higher forms of beauty, or exercising the finer qualities of moral attitude (as, for example, acceptance of responsibility and inward determination to do the right because it is seen to be right), we see at once that these cannot be compelled. No teacher could for a moment think to threaten his students that they must under penalty of punishment appreciate Gray's "Elegy" by a certain named day. Appreciation comes not so, but only in any true or effective sense as the learner himself sees in the poem that which truly evokes his appreciation. I as master or friend may help a learner to look at, and perhaps to see, such things as do commonly evoke appreciation. But compel his appreciation I cannot; it is impossible.

The same is true of any moral act or attitude. The situation as seen by the learner must be such that it, as he confronts it, stirs in him this moral-quality response. The law or the authority of a master may compel the outward act of seeming regret or repentance, as the saying of certain words or the outward performance of certain deeds, but the inner attitude may be very different from this outer act. This inner quality which alone constitutes the true quality of moral attitude lies beyond compulsion. It may be encouraged and it may be cultivated. It cannot be compelled.

This means that where spiritual values are at stake, teaching must cease to be dictating and come to be guiding. Guiding on a democratic and spiritual basis means that we start where the child is (there is nowhere else to start effectively) and get the best in him going as best we can, and then help him grow.

Since no one lives to himself, we work with children in groups
—especially so after nursery school days—and use the group
as constructively as we can to help create the high quality of
living we seek.

We seek then that living among youth as will furnish such
situations as inherently call forth, as best possible, responses fit
to be lived and learned. The social situation properly guided
is, we believe, the most favorable for this. The spiritual values
we seek are all either directly or indirectly social in character.
Even the least social—as, say, the personal appreciation of a
sunset—is often the more appreciated as others discuss it and
share the enjoyment. The social situation, if adequately
steered, is then the specially favorable milieu in which to learn
spiritual values. Group approval stimulates the arising of individual responses to fit; and if unfit responses come, as at
times they may, the judgment of one's fellows against one is
the surest available means for bringing the needed inner repentance. There is no place where the teacher's part can be
more socially significant than in steering the joint work of
pupils. What is undertaken by these must, when tried, actually
carry in them its own inherent motivation. Otherwise we are
back again on the basis of external compulsion or, what may
be just as bad, on the basis of *laissez faire* where each acts in
selfish disregard of common goals. The teacher must act positively to help steer the common process *from within* to *its own
best* ends. When such guidance is tactfully wise both in the
choice of ends and in the carrying forward of choices made,
the young will surprise us by their seriousness of effort and
pertinence of thought. But in it all the active social situation is
typically the necessary one.

There are yet greater depths to the action of this social-
group factor. Whatever has long been consistently accepted in
the social history of a group, as, for example, the rejection of
incest, so builds the institutional life and attitudes about itself
that merely to grow up normally in that social group is for

the ordinary human sufficient to in-build the appropriate attitudes in him almost beyond the possibility of temptation to the contrary. It is in this way that many of the strongest actual elements of human character are built. Bravery in the face of danger is one such; hardly will one brought up in our culture consent to be thought a coward. Patriotism is another. Of course such inevitable results carry their dangers, as the history of bravery and patriotism in Germany and Japan suffice to show, but the process of learning is no less well illustrated.

In this respect, it seems that somehow the British historic background has proved capable of developing an unusually resistant strength of character. The bombing of London not only did not suffice to shake this strength, it seemed actually to call it forth for still more effective action; and this not only at the specific point of bombing, but wherever the need might be. The surest way then to build the needed spiritual strength into the character and behavior of the rising generation is for the surrounding adult generation to live that strength so consistently in all their dealings with the young that these will see its value and grow up accepting it. If it is a really needed spiritual quality that is thus taught, living it will not only teach it, it will also justify it by the felt results it brings forth in the quality of living realized. To expect such complete supporting behavior from adults would, of course, be beyond reason. But the principle nevertheless carries positive demands for parents and teachers and, besides, sets forth a definite ideal for the community. Our youth will learn what they live; we elders must do our part that they may live well.

Building Conceptions, Attitudes, Habits. As we consider any roster of spiritual values such as those suggested earlier, it appears that the ultimately desirable form or state of each such incarnate value can, at least for the most part, be reached only as the organized accumulation of many successive learnings. It appears further that each such embodied value has typically three component aspects, a conceptional or intellectual aspect, a conative or wish or attitudinal aspect, and a physical action aspect.[7] In any particular instance one component may stand out as if it alone were present, but closer inspection will show the other two present at least by implication. Thus respect for personality may be predominantly an attitude; but as an attitude it would be blind indeed if it carried no adequate thought content to help tell what form the respect should take according to the particular situation at hand. And the respect would further be immorally futile if as an attitude it could feel for others but could in no wise put feeling into action.

These three named component aspects appear as such in the title of this section. The question is how to build them, build them as it were, separately, yet so interrelated that they can and will work together as they must in life.

Each one when he responds, to summarize, responds (at least typically) "all over"; that is, he thinks, he feels, he moves physically. And he does these three as nearly simultaneous but overlapping component aspects of each response. It is this overlapping-simultaneous complexity of response which gives us here the key to the desired building, the building alike of each named component and of the needed interrelatedness of the

[7] It must be clearly understood that these "component aspects" do not have prior and independent existence. They are not to be thought of as separate things combined here to make up the value under consideration. Any actual spiritual value exists, organically, as a personal behavior pattern available as a resource ready to be called usefully into play when appropriate occasion may offer. When the organism does so respond, any interested on-looker—including the person himself—may for his purposes recognize thinking as one aspect of the behavior act, a wishing tendency as another aspect, and a physical moving as a third. An accompanying internal glandular secretion is a frequent fourth. The advantage for thought and practice of singling out such component aspects for separate consideration has been amply justified in our cultural history. Our world of thought and thoughtful action has in fact been built on the psychological possibility of abstracting out for study component items from a concrete whole. Perversions of the practice in philosophical systems are no sufficient reason for denying its possible proper use.

three if they are on each occasion of use to act together as they must and do.

One's conception of any matter or thing is one's idea of the possible behavior of that thing. In origin, it is the organized aggregate of all one's successive thoughts and thought experiences of the thing. Such a conception, it needs hardly be said, is quite different from the Aristotelian concept, which dealt largely with clear-cut boundaries embracing internal homogeneity. My conception of anything constitutes then my present expectation of what I can experience in connection with that thing; it is my mental orientation to that thing. Thus my conception of a horse is fuller and much more explicit than my conception of a zebra, my life experience of horses having been far more abundant and more exacting than of zebras. These experiences in both cases have been organized by me largely through use for use. In each case, as befits our earlier discussions, learning through living for living has built the conception.

It is similar to my conception of any spiritual value, say, of respect for personality. It too has been built through use and for use. Though this conception lies, relatively speaking, in what we often call the abstract rather than the concrete world, the actual facts of respect rather than disrespect lie deep down in the concrete world, as any child can feel even though he lacks words for describing the difference. Farther along the road toward maturity lie the consciously named conceptions of personality and respect for personality. As so named, these particular conceptions can be built only by those far enough advanced to think in some measure critically both of what they do and of how they describe it. Discernible differences of actual treatment, however, implied in the term *respect for personality* will, as suggested, begin in early childhood. Parents and teachers must be keenly aware that children do begin early to feel such distinctions, and must take every care to be thoughtful and consistent in their consequent treatment of the young under their care. A double obligation holds here, the one to treat the child considerately, the other to help him make defensible distinctions in the area. The building of valid and usable distinctions so as to promote thinking in connection is the indispensable foundation for spiritual growth. Nothing can be more important. The appropriate use of names is an important feature here. A suitable name even on the childish level helps to fix a distinction; and on such distinctions later experiences can build the accumulations necessary for more adequate conceptions. The organization of such accumulations, it seems, is best built on the consistent use of terms, and here thoughtful elders are necessary. As adolescence comes on, increasing practice in the critical discussion of such terms will help greatly in the building of still more adequate conceptions.

A somewhat analogous discussion holds for building attitudes. Indeed, one significant part of any properly defensible attitude is a discriminating conception of the object of the attitude. How I should feel toward anything, how I should feel disposed to act toward that thing, will differ according to conditions. The different conditions under which I can face any given thing must then be built as discriminating constituents into my conception of that thing; otherwise I can have no properly discriminative attitude toward it. As teacher I must feel toward each child under me an attitude of definite and persistent good will. But this good will must be discriminating. Certain tendencies in Henry I must watch as possible dangers, other tendencies I must foster to upbuild with every care, still others will—relatively speaking—take care of themselves. In a word, I must know Henry as well as I can in order to be wise in my good will toward him; and this "knowing" is exactly the conception here discussed.

Our problem, however, is that of helping the child and the youth to build the proper attitudes, and in this the feeling-impulse aspect is the dominant feature. It is how I feel and what accordingly I am disposed to do that counts in my spiritual life. The proper attitude toward a complex object in a complex and precarious world is itself complex and this is especially true of spiritual attitudes. So our discussion had better begin with the simpler and more concrete instances and go on later to the more complex spiritual values.

In the childhood of him who writes these words open wood fires in wooden houses was the rule. To build in the young the proper attitudes of caution where fire was involved was an early and urgent necessity, caution that the child himself not get burned, caution with his toys and household objects that they not be burned, caution that the fire not get out of the fireplace and burn down the house. As for the child himself, reliance was given to the old rule "a burnt child dreads the fire"; carefully managed experiences of fire supplemented by accidental burns sufficed to teach this caution. As for toys and more valuable household objects, seeing how fire did in fact consume taught the facts, while a general sense of value arising out of enforced frugality did the rest. As for the house, the obviously serious and definitely repeated fears of parents gave to this an early and urgent importance. The three factors here at work are (1) "how it feels to you," (2) what consequences can be objectively expected, and (3) how others feel. These three give us perhaps the main reliance in building actual attitudes in the young in every area.

A certain amount of direct experience is prerequisite to attitude building in all three realms of "the true, the beautiful, and the good." In the moral realm, if consistency and kindliness rule and not too rapid progress is demanded, the child can usually be led, and easily, from how he feels to how others feel and so, first, to acceptance of reasonable rules of behavior for himself in relation to others and then, second, to acceptance of responsibility to make the better way prevail in the group. For both steps, wisely led group approval is a great help, in fact practically a necessity. In the matter of responsibility, as the younger group members grow older they easily take pleasure in showing the newcomers "how we do it here." These are beginning steps toward building moral and ethical attitudes. Consistency of action and an increasing understanding of the reason why may be counted on as the promising ways of strengthening such attitudes.

As to beginnings in the aesthetic realm, whether of reading or of "art" or of music, the chief thing seems to be not to stress externally imposed mechanics to the hurt of personal activity or of understanding or appreciation. In reading, as is later suggested, there is great danger of pushing this upon unready minds. To push a child faster than he can go is the surest way to build hurtful attitudes. Interest too, as it emerges, is individual and must be respected as such if it is to be best cultivated. Analogous suggestions seem to hold for music and art; the more surely the child can be satisfactorily active, the surer can we hope for growth. To say these things does not mean that guidance to richer experience and to more adequate technique is not needed—the contrary is most true. But always the next step must lie where the child now is; and always the forward step must be the fullest use, by the child, of powers he now has; and the more self-directive and creative he can be to make progress and the more surely such efforts meet observable success, the surer is the learner building the desirable attitudes with respect to his work. Stimulation to advance may, perhaps, come mainly from without; but the advance itself must come from within—from within the child and his present powers of reconstruction, from within the area of experience already felt to be in hand.

It is the accumulation, the co-ordination, and the refinement of these beginning attitudes that constitute growth in the spiritual realm. As an aggregate is thus built of interactive parts, strength is built; for each part will reinforce the rest and all will support any area as it feels attack from without.

No separate discussion is here given of attitudes regarding "the true." The like discussion to the preceding would hold. Nor is separate treatment given to the building of specific habits. Again the like treatment would hold if only the matter be carried sufficiently into action.

As we seek to cultivate spiritual qualities in the young, we must not, as earlier suggested, overlook the essential factor of psychological "readiness" before a new line of experience is definitely taken up. Our better schools have learned this with regard to the ordinary fields of study. If the child be forced into reading or number work or literary appreciation or group co-operation or a certain moral advance before he is psychologically ready for it, the evil result will often extend far beyond the mere temporary failure to accomplish the assigned task. Discouragement may bring such feelings of inferiority and such "emotional" reluctance to attack again that type of work with zest and confidence as can result in the worst instances in a certain emotional stupidity, so to say, in the failed area. The older school methods, correlative of a set-out-in-advance course of study, have here many sins to answer for. These considerations hold with peculiar force wherever spiritual values are involved.

Our social inheritance must furnish the main source for individual growth in these spiritually needed conceptions, attitudes, and habits. And guidance here, let it be repeated, is necessary in order that these spiritual riches may be adequately utilized. Part of this needed guidance may indeed be impersonal, as the very common use of a word may serve as stimulus to the young to ask its meaning and seek its use. Or a custom, as the universal rising at the national anthem, may demand personal conformity when sufficient age is reached. But even these instances are as a rule personally steered; and, besides, there is always the danger that words and customs will be learned only outwardly and so with no adequate spiritual quality in the use. The necessary personal guidance and stimulation must come from those who themselves feel the richness involved—and the more numerous these can be, the better. Otherwise the young may grow up to a wholly inadequate appropriation of the spiritual riches potentially awaiting them. Indeed, with even the best reared it generally proves necessary during adolescence to re-examine, re-think, and re-accept (or discriminatingly reject) the spiritual inheritance adopted in youth. As children we usually learn inadequately; when we grow older we must put away childish ideas. At this stage, of course, the guidance has to be unusually tactful for the older adolescent has to become independent. But a sufficiently wise guidance can still prove helpful, if not essential.

Emotion and Spiritual Values. The part played by feeling or emotion in building spiritual values has been implicit in all so far said. We have seen more than once how the organism acts, typically if not always, "as a whole." Feeling enters thus in some degree in all significant experience and is presumably an element in all behavior showing the spiritual quality. It is the different ways in which emotion significantly affects the spiritual quality of life that here concern us.

First in time and perhaps in importance is the place of emotion in "personality adjustment." We can hardly expect a healthy attitude toward spiritual values where there is serious "emotional maladjustment." The building of a well-adjusted personality becomes then the first and underlying task in any program to foster spiritual values. Naturally this begins in the home, with the mother as the chief factor at work. She must first of all wish the expected child and then must protect and guide him with loving care through the vicissitudes of child life. She must accordingly be sensitive alike to all the child's growing feelings and to the needed ethical and cultural characteristics of the good life. Her own family life with her ideals and her effective tact are here essential factors.

The school is the next most important factor in building personality adjustment. The general tone of the school is here strategic. School work unsuited to child nature or to personal readiness, rigidity of curriculum, autocratic discipline, competitive marks and report cards—all such are the conditions which may make for maladjustment. Positively, the school must work, democratically, for ever more adequate self-direction in the light of ever better-seen demands for the social good. Loyalties to the spiritual values must be built on the basis of the ever better-seen inherent needs for such values and not on the basis of indoctrination, however skillfully imposed. It is life the school must seek, life of a quality leading naturally to personality unfolding based on the desired spiritual values.

Feeling as such plays also an inherent role in the learning of spiritual values. We learn what we live. Emotion or feeling resulting in refined and discriminating sentiments would seem the very essence of the spiritual quality here sought. For man to rise above the brute he must see and enjoy mental discriminations and generalization of a high order. Added to this, the emotional soul of the learner must go out in active appreciation and acceptance of the refined distinctions thus mentally made. Otherwise the spiritual values are not lived and the desired learning and soul building will not take place. Only as spiritual quality is felt can it be learned. Out of the heart are the issues of life.

Home and school must then both successively and simultaneously work along these lines. Spiritual values have to be individually built, but they are seldom individually devised— at least not in childhood and youth. The race-wrought spiritual heritage must be the source of learnings, and for this parent and teacher are essential. The child will learn distinctions only as he lives them, and he will live them only as his shared life with others who are farther along turns on these distinctions. When the home lives certain distinctions, whether of thought or behavior, the child must—at the appropriate age—learn these distinctions if he is to share adequately in the common home life. The school a little later must rely upon the same shared living to get its most important lessons learned. And still later the living must under proper guidance reach steadily farther into the ever enlarging surrounding community. It is only as children and youth have the advantage of sharing life with others who embody the spiritual values that we can hope to see the needed spiritual values widely learned.

CONCLUSION

This discussion can be briefly summed up. Spiritual values have in fact to be lived or they will not be so learned as to get effectively into life. It is possible to memorize words about values and then to learn to use the values in living.

We may repeat the same principle but in other words. The needed spiritual values can be lived—and so learned—only under such conditions as call forth in the learning soul the desired values as the response of that soul to actual conditions of life as confronted.

Only as life is thus lived can we hope that our youth—and our citizens—will learn the spiritual values needed to make life fine and good.

Chapter VII

SCHOOL PRACTICE AND SPIRITUAL VALUES—I

EVERY teacher has spiritual effect on his pupils in many ways. Pupils learn from him to value certain things and to disregard or reject others. He influences their personality, their outlook on life, their attitudes toward themselves and toward others, their disposition to build a world better for all, their ability to help in the building, their techniques of doing so. Teachers have been, however, on the whole more accustomed to think of their responsibility to the child in terms of subject matter, of knowledge to be imparted, than of the spiritual values simultaneously at stake. Because these latter values may have effects for the child and for society in many cases more important and far-reaching than the subjects learned, it is essential for teachers to think in these terms and to keep in mind that pupils are constantly learning for good or ill along all these lines. To ignore what is thus being learned will not prevent the learning, it will only make it go on less well, and perhaps negatively rather than positively.

If the teacher is to meet this responsibility adequately, he will need to have clearly in mind specific values which are at stake so that he may constantly evaluate his procedures and the school practices with reference to them. Does this mean that he will decide on a set of aims important to him and seek to indoctrinate the children with them? Some teachers, of course, do exactly that. But he will not do it if one of his aims is to aid his pupils to become free men. It is unrealistic, however, to assume that failure to be aware of and to stress some values rather than others will protect pupils from undue influence and will therefore insure their freedom to choose. On the contrary, their very inexperience and ignorance may close doors to them. The safeguard lies not in ignoring and keeping hands off, but in examining and choosing to stress values which really lead the pupils toward conscious control over their own lives. What, then, are some of these values which build toward freedom, which foster the spiritual in life?

SOME SPIRITUAL VALUES THE SCHOOL SHOULD SEEK

An inclusive list of values, and especially a list to which all could subscribe, would, of course, be an impossibility. As discussed in Chapter II, however, there are certain values strategic to spiritual living on which most thoughtful people would agree. Some of these values, discussed there in connection with the community, will be restated here for purposes of continuity and discussed in terms of their interrelations with school practice.

Respect for Personality. First in any list of values strategic to democracy and to spirituality is respect for persons, a sense of their dignity and worth which requires that they be treated as ends, not means merely, as individuals with feelings and preferences and desires, with potentialities to be developed. Each individual, whatever his past experience, is entitled to the respect due a human being and to the opportunity to feel self-respect and self-confidence. He is entitled to opportunity to set up ends, to exercise initiative, to have his own thoughts and opinions. He is entitled to the right to grow to his best, to become the finest human being he is able to become, to live the fullest life he is capable of living. Richness or poorness, beauty or ugliness, high ability or low ability, great contribution to society or lesser contribution, fortunate past or unfortunate— none of these negate our responsibility to treat him as a person and help him to become his best.

But as we owe these things to each human being, so he also owes them to all others. As a participant in democratic living he must respect others, show consideration of their rights. He must build and increasingly act on the conception that as he is entitled to respect and consideration, so is each other person entitled to similar respect and consideration, to courteous treatment, to his own thoughts, feelings, values. This means, of course, tolerance of others' points of view; but mere tolerance is too negative to suffice. It means also, positively, sympathetic understanding and treatment of others, insuring them fairness, justice, opportunity to be themselves, to exercise initiative, to work out their own destiny in so far as it does not harm others.

The two, then, go together—right of the individual to respect and consideration so long as he does not affect others adversely, and responsibility of the individual to see that each other also receives this respect and consideration. To build a conception of such treatment, to expect it for himself and to accord it to others, to build increasingly a conception of group life on this basis and to build determination that such group life shall prevail—this is to build the most strategic conception in democracy and one of the most strategic spiritual values.

Increasing Control over One's Own Destiny. A democratic school will seek in season and out to help pupils to exercise increasing control over their own destiny. No one whose framework of living is controlled importantly by others can taste life to the full, can attain the full spiritual stature of a free man. To increase such control, then, means increasing self-directiveness on the part of the pupil, increasing disposition to take responsibility for himself and skill in doing so, and increasing ability to make choices which will be counted good in the long run. It means development of his own initiative so he need not be at the mercy of others' direction. It means development of and use of his own intelligence, his own ideas and conceptions and resources, his own techniques of reasoning; it means the building up of his own mind (versus the habit of relying on others to think for him), the building of his own opinions and values (versus the disposition to accept, to swallow the ideas of others). But it equally means growing knowledge to be utilized in exercising control—knowledge of what others have found out and, importantly, knowledge of the world today, of forces and movements and situations to be taken into account and resources to be utilized. Growing knowledge, it can scarcely be too strongly stressed, is an indispensable essential to growth in the qualities mentioned above, for example, self-directiveness, carrying responsibility, developing the individual's own mind.

Ability to control one's destiny means, still further, growing knowledge of the techniques of effecting—effecting by one's self and effecting with others in that large number of situations where co-operative effort is indicated if common purposes are to be realized.

Loyalty to Democratic Group Life. It is of the essence of both democracy and spirituality to strive for a group life in which each, as indicated above, can have his own thoughts, feelings, values, can feel himself respected and valued, and this in spite of variations from dominant patterns. But, in addition, individuals in the group should see that right to respect and freedom to have one's own values indicate the correlative obligation to maintain a situation in which all, himself and each other, can have the same privilege. To do less is selfish and, moreover, a failure to see the deeper meaning of democracy. To build, then, a recognition of the right and necessity of being ourselves, of maintaining our own integrity, with all that is implied, is to build only one part of the conception essential to the realization of this value. A more searching criterion of attachment to democracy, in its most spiritual aspect, is loyalty to a way of life which recognizes, values, and strives for the good life for all, loyalty to the effort to build a finer world in which all may have conditions of life to enable them to live and work effectively.

Similarly basic in democratic group life is loyalty to the free play of intelligence as a method, a method both of determining the values of others and of finding the most effective ways of realizing them. When some cannot be heard, their values will be discounted or ignored. When some sorts of proposals cannot receive consideration, our stock of ideas is less rich, less likely to be effective in improving the quality of life for all. Loyalty, then, to the free play of intelligence and the disposition to rely on it is a fundamentally spiritual value.

Aesthetic Sensitivities and Enjoyments. "No democrat is willing that any human being should go through his years on earth without being stirred by beauty, excited by meaning, challenged and aroused by perplexing endeavor."[1] Few discerning democrats will wish to take issue with this statement. Acceptance of it places on us the obligation to strive for conditions in which realization of the implied aim is encouraged. Drab schoolrooms, living and teaching methods devoid of encouragement to creativeness, curricula restricted to utilitarian and mechanical pursuits—these deny development of this essentially spiritual quality. On the other hand, enterprises which call forth love and beauty and skill in producing it, joyousness in putting creative effort into what is felt to be meaningful, worth while, satisfying—these give aesthetic enjoyments which both constitute their own immediate justification and simultaneously build a cumulative resource for continuing satisfaction and enjoyment. Such enjoyments may be found, for example, in the arts, in carpentry, in child rearing, in research, in social action, in satisfying relationships with people; they may be found in any activity with potentialities for stirring human purposes and ingenuity, for bringing to bear —at any level—thoughtful, discriminating evaluation and satisfaction in what is done. William James, stressing the range of possibilities and the values to be achieved, rather than the necessary conditions, has said it this way:

[1] Alexander Meiklejohn, *What Does America Mean?* (New York: W. W. Norton & Company, 1935), p. 198.

Wherever a process of life communicates an eagerness to him who lives it, there the life becomes genuinely significant. Sometimes the eagerness is more knit up with the motor activities, sometimes with the perceptions, sometimes with the imagination, sometimes with reflective thought. But, wherever it is found, there is the zest, the tingle, the excitement of reality; and there *is* "importance" in the only real and positive sense in which importance ever anywhere can be.[2]

This, the eagerness, zest, tingle in life, is surely what every spiritually sensitive person should wish for every other person.

Moral Fiber. By moral fiber is meant willingness to undertake what is hard, once it has been decided to be good, and to go through with the steps necessary to attain it with satisfaction in the conviction that though it is not easy it is nevertheless worth while. It means persistence, tenacity of purpose, the disposition to stick to what one believes is right, to see it through in spite of difficulties, obstacles, inconvenience, discouragement. It does not mean sticking, like the boy on the burning deck, in spite of wisdom to the contrary. It is the exact opposite of capricious shifting about, of yielding to temptations of ease, of yielding to dissuasion by those insensitive to the values at stake. It means ability to take into account not merely one's own interests but also the effects of one's acts on others and to hold oneself to concern with these wider values. It means ability to look ahead, plan, and work out in terms of long-run values rather than mere concern with the immediate.

To build such moral fiber is essential both to realization of the individual's own best interests and to the welfare of the group. It is an aspect of every character justly called spiritual.

HOW DOES THE TEACHER HELP IN THE BUILDING OF VALUES?

The teacher must, in the first place, have clearly in mind the values he cherishes and wishes to further, the philosophy of life he stands for. Even a teacher who is ignorant of or

[2] *Talks to Teachers* (New York: Henry Holt & Company, 1900), p. 234.

rejects the terms *value* and *philosophy of life* has nevertheless explicit impact on pupils in terms of certain values. He influences them out of what he believes in. Though he has not examined what he believes and has no plant to introduce it into the teaching situation, he acts out of his pattern of belief. For example, he treats the children democratically or autocratically; he makes them feel they are important as persons or unimportant except as cogs in the wheel, as able to make choices or inadequate to do so; he has effect in encouraging them to stand on their own feet or the reverse. All this whether he is aware of it or not. No person is without his beliefs and attitudes, his personality pattern, his "philosophy," out of which he acts more or less consistently and out of which he affects others in dealing with them.

The teacher has accordingly an obligation to examine his philosophy, to be aware that he does affect others, and to build for himself an examined, criticized, *chosen* set of values, rather than to act haphazardly and unconsciously. He should scrutinize his practices and the school practices for their effect on the personality being built by the pupils and should decide whether the effects are ones he wishes to take responsibility for, ones he wishes to see built into the lives of the people he influences, ones he wishes to see incorporated into the fabric of our society.

Individual teachers will, of course, return different answers to this questioning, depending on their background of experience, their insight, their entire cluster of value patterns. This discussion, however, is written out of the assumption that most people in this country wish democracy and wish—if they are aware—their acts to build toward that end. If this basic assumption is not accepted, a set of aims different from the ones proposed will be set up. For people in autocracy one might wish moral fiber—to be utilized for autocratic ends. One might wish aesthetic experiences of a sort, but not for persons to be creative in all types of experience. The other values listed point immediately and unmistakably in the direction of democracy. The discussion is, then, avowedly based on the assumption of a preference for and choice of democracy as a way of life to be sought.

Is it consistent, it may be asked, to choose a way of life to build in other people and to indicate, simultaneously, that each should be helped to control his own destiny? The answer is yes, if the aim for the individual to build increasing control over his own life is kept constantly in mind. The teacher will then, when he presses for even so basic a value as democracy, do it in a way to help pupils to think more adequately about it for themselves, become more intelligently critical about it. For the teacher to work toward an end and simultaneously to increase ability in the pupil to evaluate the end is not inconsistent or impossible. And the ends listed are ones which assume and point toward control over one's own life and thought processes. One strand in the teacher's aims at every point will, accordingly, be to increase the pupil's ability to do his own thinking, to become increasingly less dependent on the direction of the teacher or of others, and at the same time increasingly aware of facts and values to be taken into account and of the effects of his acts on his own living and on the living of others.

How, then, does the teacher take account of his values as he carries on his work with his pupils? As he plans for the group, as he considers his total aims for them, as he faces and works through each situation, he first of all keeps in mind his basic values. (This is not to say he takes them out every morning; for a person who has brought his values to definite consciousness and made them an inherent part of his thinking no special effort to keep them in mind is necessary; each thoughtful use of them, however, should aid in their re-evaluation.) The teacher considers, for example, what he wishes for these pupils —that they develop as persons, with self-confidence, with resources, with opinions, and also with consideration for others; that their right to grow be fostered, rather than allowing them chiefly to repeat what they have done before; that they develop also in ability to manage their own living, become self-directing, build up their own minds, learn techniques for working together effectively; that they grow in knowledge and insight into the world around them; and so on. How can he best accomplish these ends?

Suppose, for example, a teacher is planning for a group of young children. Shall I, he asks, leave the children to their own devices, in the thought that this will best help them to realize themselves as persons? The answer is emphatically no; with their immaturity and ignorance, that would not most respect their potentialities. They come with different backgrounds of experience which dispose some to be timid, some to be domineering. They come from different backgrounds of home and community living which have taught them conflicting and perhaps unfruitful ways of behaving. They would tend to behave the ways they have learned before—some aggressively, some unsocially, some timidly, but all in the ways they are accustomed to. The ways some choose to behave may disregard others and make life unhappy for them. The timid ones may withdraw into themselves or have experiences with the others which make them even less secure. If I want them to grow, to have more resources, they need opportunity and encouragement to be busy with fruitful activities. I must see that the necessary materials and conditions for such activities are provided. If I want them to learn consideration for others, I must help them to act considerately, to note what considerate treatment of themselves means, to wish to treat others similarly. I must see that in their experiences together they become more sensitive to the feelings and needs of others and that they take these increasingly into account in their acts. I must help them feel that to respect others' needs is important. If I want them to learn to manage their own living, I must help them to do it successfully; for ability to manage one's own living effectively is *learned*. I must not force ideas on them in a way to stifle their own, and I must not so take over the making of decisions that they do not learn how to make their own and to value their own judgment. On the contrary, I must help *them* to make choices, as wise choices as they are capable of making, which take into account whatever they are able to see in effects on their own living and on that of others; I must help them to make wiser choices than they would be able to make without my mature help. I must help them in ways they could not help themselves and in ways their environment otherwise may not teach them unless it is sensitive to the more spiritual aspects of living.

Or, to take another situation, how shall this sixth grade be managed so that the orderly living, study, and work essential to the growing of all can go on and so the pupils will build moral fiber through the experience? The teacher may consider as follows: To keep control exclusively in my hands would insure order but it would not help them to grow in ability to order their own lives, to control themselves. I must, then, combine the two aims, to have order and to increase the children's sense of responsibility, so that I make them at the same time less dependent on me and more disposed to manage themselves wisely.

How, also, shall I manage so that the pupils build the good study and work habits essential to accomplishment? Can they, for example, make an intelligent plan and hold themselves persistently to its accomplishment? Or do they need help with this? Are their study and work habits building in them the disposition to be satisfied with the easy only, or are they willing to attack the difficult, to put forth real effort, to stick at it and see enterprises through in spite of difficulties? Do they recognize and meet obligations, or do they ignore them or make excuses? And, from another angle, are their tasks suited to them—challenging but meaningful and manageable? The answer is important, for stumbling through meaningless and hopeless tasks builds discouragement, disinclination to try, lack of belief in one's self—the reverse of what goes to make up moral fiber. The facts turned up by this exploration give clues to lines of help the pupils need and to the teacher's own responsibility.

Or, in still another situation, the teacher may face a different sort of problem: How shall I teach these high school pupils about the French Revolution? Or indeed *shall* I teach them about it? The area is one closely related to the development of democratic living, about which I want them to be informed, and the period—to those who grasp its significance—is a crucial and stirring one in the world's history. I want the pupils to gain perspective on their own times, to have background for their own thinking. I want them increasingly to be able to see present events in terms of the situations and happenings out of which they have evolved. From this point of view study of the French Revolution has important potentialities. I would much like to have pupils study it if the effects will be the positive ones mentioned, and not largely negative.

But can I make such study meaningful to them so they can utilize it understandingly in their own thinking? I prefer *not* to teach it if the study will result only in accumulation of dates, facts, items of information meaningless to the pupils, with no real relation they can see to their lives. In that case, the study would violate spirituality by dulling their desire to learn, by making them more disposed to swallow facts, less disposed to think about what they do.

For some pupils an understanding of the French Revolution may be, in truth, the least pressing of their needs. For pupils with meager knowledge and effectiveness in life around them, with a limited store of conceptions to think with, for pupils with little taste for books, with no experience in dealing with ideas except to memorize them, this may be exactly the wrong topic to carry them farther along. Study of a topic as remote in time and space as the French Revolution may be teaching them to disregard and escape from their own problems, to feel all one can do in schools is to repeat the words of others. It may reinforce their conception that study is *reading about* the remote, rather than finding how to meet life around them. It may teach them to hate books and study because they see no meaning in them. With some pupils intelligent methods may help to bridge the gap. But it must in all honesty be recognized that good method will not suffice to compensate for conceptions and abilities and attitudes which need to be built first so that more complex conceptions and situations can be grasped and utilized fruitfully. If this class is such a group, respect for them as persons demands that I help them with their more important needs (for example, learning to be at home with books, learning to use their own minds on something real to them, learning to attack the problems of living in their own community, getting a conception of the meaning of freedom in the lives of men they know which may be built on increasingly). Respect for personality demands that I start where they are and help them to grow in ways that will make them more curious, insightful, happy, effective in their own life situations.

But for a different sort of group, study of the French Revolution may make a great contribution to their growth in insight into the life and times they live in, it may help them significantly to control the processes of their developing community life more intelligently. To see how the struggles of others have helped to bring into being the ideas and conditions of liberty we take for granted, to see how group alignments and happenings in the French Revolution are still embedded in the situation in France today, to see how, then, our own welfare is tied up with the development of events in France earlier and in France today—such insights (quite different from memorization of unrelated facts) can be both thrilling and illuminating to present living and thinking. With any class whose experiences have been such that they can grasp the meanings in the study and use them to think with (versus merely memorize and verbalize), study of the French Revolution offers many possibilities for extending their conceptions. If the group is mature, socially and intellectually, and has learned to work effectively with historical materials, it may even be ready for intensive and systematic study of the period and its interrelations. The test in each case will be the way the study takes hold in the minds of the pupils, the way they grasp its meanings and relate these to life about them.

It should be apparent that teacher-pupil planning, both of what is to be studied and of how to work at what is chosen, will be of tremendous help to the teacher in seeing his way through this exploration, as well as of great advantage otherwise in the learning of the pupils. When teacher and pupil examine jointly the possibilities involved, make an initial sortie into the proposed territory, it becomes much easier to predict how the study will take hold, what connections with life about them pupils will make. In addition, if the pupils take joint responsibility for the decision, positive attitudes rather than negative will contribute their share to success. If, on the other hand, the school allows no leeway in choosing, the entire exploration becomes meaningless except as a stimulus to thinking about method.

The teacher, then, must weigh the various questions: Can I manage so they will come out with more ideas of their own to think with, with insights they did not have before, with increased ability to think for themselves, to use and develop their own minds? Or is the French Revolution so remote from their lives that working at it will strike no spark, communicate no meanings, allow them no possibility of thinking for themselves? Will the materials take hold so they can work at it with zest and eagerness and creativeness? Or will they work mechanically and in a purblind fashion which will dull their curiosity and eagerness to learn? Will the study add to understanding of life as they see it and live it? Will it help them to live more enjoyably or more effectively? Will it add to their appreciation of and loyalty to democratic group life? The answers to these questions have real spiritual import.

The foregoing discussion has considered how the teacher in his planning, in his facing of situations, brings into play his set of values. But the teacher also wishes to help his pupils to build considered values. He wishes this lest they too act haphazardly and out of unexamined and unconscious assumptions and so fail of spiritual development and behavior.

How does the teacher help in the building of values? In the first place he keeps in mind that the pupil learns what he lives-thinks-feels-accepts and that the experiences most real to him, closest to life as he sees it, are the ones he lives-thinks-feels-accepts most deeply. The teacher therefore recognizes that the pupil's actual life experiences, those he identifies himself with most thoroughly, are the crucial ones for character and value building. He accordingly watches the day-to-day situations, in living about the school and in study-work-class experiences, to observe how living goes on, the "values" out of which the pupils act, the conceptions of spiritual import which they use. From these observations he gets clues as to their needs for more adequate conceptions. When such needs are revealed he strives along several lines: to make the living go on better so the pupils may live the value to be taken into account; to help the pupils become increasingly conscious of the values inherent in their behavior; to help them criticize and evaluate the value-conception and increasingly accept it to act on consciously and critically. With younger children the first two processes may be carried out more satisfactorily than the other two. With older pupils critical evaluation and conscious acceptance must be a necessary part of the learning if they are not to learn to act blindly.

With younger children, then, the teacher strives to make the situation one in which the living can exemplify the proper values—to see, for example, that sufficient toys are available for each to have a chance at them and so not put a premium on snatching toys away from others; to see that sufficient space is available to reduce the tensions caused by too crowded conditions. When toy-snatching does go on he helps the child to get the idea of *mine* and *hers*, but he also provides something satisfactory for both. He strives, too, to help the children become increasingly aware of fairness as a conception—he helps them to get a name for the instance if they do not connect one with it. For with young children a name for what is involved helps to call attention to the idea, to enter a beginning wedge, a nucleus of meaning around which more extended meanings can accumulate and crystallize. He helps the children also to see how fairness feels to themselves and so to playmates, to differentiate fairness from unfairness in the situations about them, and, to the extent that they are able, to evaluate the relative satisfactions of fair and unfair behavior. ("If everybody snatched toys none of us could play in peace.") He keeps in mind that the child who is to accept fairness as a value must feel in his own mind that fairness as a way of dealing works out well. As the days go by he helps the children to see other instances of fairness (in games, taking turns, doing one's just share, giving an objective account of what happens, and so on) so they can build a more adequate and inclusive conception of what fairness involves and increasingly evaluate its merits.

With older pupils much the same process goes on. They, however, may be farther along in definiteness of conceptions and so able to talk about the principles involved; they may be mature enough to discuss the abstract ideas as well as the concrete situations. They will have had more experiences to think with and to illuminate discussion. But if their experiences have not taught them defensible conceptions, they need help in exactly the same ways as younger children—help in making their living situations the kind to encourage acting-and-accepting the better way, help in becoming aware of the value-conception and in evaluating its worth, increasing encouragement to digest its meaning and to accept it consciously to act on, help in generalizing the meanings and seeing their application in a wider variety of situations.

The teacher should stand ready to give help at any point as needed. It should, however, be made explicit that mere exhorting will not build valuing in a pupil. (It may instead hinder.) The pupil must make his own positive responses to the value if he is to learn it. Nor will mere naming or verbalizing of itself build a value. On the contrary, acting on it is fundamentally essential. The teacher should therefore differentiate clearly the purposes to be served by terminology and the fact that verbalizing, talking *about* fairness, is different from the acting-and-feeling fairness process discussed above.

SCHOOL PRACTICES WHICH HAVE SPIRITUAL IMPORT

As pointed out, the experiences most crucial in building children's values are the ones closest to living as they see it. Teachers may see as the important experience in the pupil's day the classes in history, mathematics, English. But to the pupil these classes may be incidents extraneous to his real living, they may in fact be scarcely experiences at all in the true sense of entering into his thinking and feeling as history, mathematics, English. What he is really experiencing may be dislike of studying and consequent rejection of school and learning situations. Or his real experiences may be other sorts of happenings about the school which he is concerned with and thinks and feels about—routines which irk him and arouse his resentment, requirements he abhors and seeks ingeniously to evade, a teacher he admires and likes to talk things over with, a teacher he despises for his sarcasm and wishes to get even with, the school play in which he has a part he likes, the campaign to raise money for football equipment which allows him to show his ability to organize and lead.

To see what a school situation is building, therefore, we must note what the children are actually living-thinking-feeling-accepting in that situation. The teacher will find here the most significant clues both as to needs in spiritual respects of the pupils themselves and as to school practices which need to be reconsidered for their spiritual effect on pupils. For many commonly accepted school practices will not stand scrutiny from the point of view of effect on pupils. Some of these practices will be examined here for their implications in character building.

Authoritarianism and Regimentation vs. Democratic Conceptions of Authority and Relationships. Perhaps the first point one notes on entering a school is where it stands on the scale of regimentation, authoritarianism, or free, joyous, democratic living. In authoritarianism decisions descend from higher to lower, with no discussion, no explanations, no recourse—the reverse of democratic decision making. Clues pointing to authoritarianism, to regimentation, frequently begin to show up even before a classroom is entered: children being marched two by two through the halls, with a teacher obviously on guard over them; sharp words at any dereliction; children in the halls only with passes; an attitude of suspicion toward anything outside the prescribed routine which communicates itself even to visitors; frequently separate doors for boys and for girls. Within the classroom: seats in rows and screwed down, all facing the teacher; no child speaks except by permission; signals given to stand or sit; all use the same books, read the same stories, write on the same topic, draw from the same model, do it when they're told, stop when they're told; the teacher is arbiter of what is right or wrong, good or bad; the teacher is the only one with freedom to initiate, with the right to opinions. In some schools the more extreme authoritarian practices give way but others remain. Pupils address teachers habitually as "sir," rise when the teacher enters or when they address teachers. Such behavior may, it is true, indicate genuine respect and desire to show courtesy, and as such it is to be valued. More often, however, in schools such behavior is designed to call attention to difference in status. Seldom, it should be noted, do we see these marks of respect and courtesy shown to pupils. In one group, then, the teachers—authority and authoritarian deciding; in the other, the pupils—carrying out orders, reproofs or penalties for failing to conform. In the one group a monopoly on origination and expression of ideas and opinions; in the other, acceptance.

What values do pupils build under a regime of regimentation or authoritarianism? It depends on what they themselves think and accept. Some rebel, outwardly and inwardly, build resentments, hatreds, rejection of authority, and worse. Others conform outwardly, as much as necessary, and inwardly indulge in clever simulation of conformity, in cynicism, in small or great deceit where it seems necessary to live their own lives, in mind-wandering in the effort to give attention where they must but with inability to shut out preoccupation with their own concerns.

Still other pupils conform outwardly and inwardly, they accept that others will tell them what to think and do and when to do it, that those in authority should not be questioned, that the "higher" tell the "lower." They accept that such procedures, being common, are proper and inevitable; they abandon the effort (or never begin) to do their own thinking or to direct their own lives. In so far as the situation succeeds they become conformists, sheep, automatons. Did the school make them so? Not the school alone; for if circumstances outside had encouraged otherwise, they might have risen above the school impact. But the school did its part; it had them for uncounted hours, days, weeks; and for many children the school was the only factor in their lives which might have taught differently. Because it did not help them to know other ways, it must bear its share of responsibility.

Did the children learn these characteristics if they did not know they were learning them and did not accept them consciously? The answer is yes; if they accepted, they were learning, though they were learning by what was chiefly conditioning. Here we have, in the case of many pupils, an instance of purblind learning, of learning negative "values." The children were not building chosen and criticized values. They were not learning to control their own destiny. They were not learning to make choices, to develop their own thinking, to take responsibility for themselves. They were not learning techniques of co-operating intelligently for the common good. Instead they were learning chiefly to follow orders. They did it day after day, because it was easier or because they had to, and for many this became their accepted way of behaving. In short, they learned living without spiritual quality.

Compare such authoritarian, regimented situations with schools in which authority is democratically derived and based on the inherent needs of the situation. Regimentation drops out. The pupils move about freely and live as individuals would in any democratic and self-regulating group situation. Teachers exercise their adult and *ex officio* authority when the situation requires it. But pupils are expected to take responsibility for themselves and are helped to learn to do so. They observe—in greater or less degree, because they are children—the restraints necessary to group living: being where they belong, being quiet when noise would interfere with the work of others, taking their turn, observing agreed-on regulations regarding use of materials, getting in work, orderly procedures, and so on. But they help in determining the regulations and procedures. They know why these are necessary, they help to pass on desirability and effectiveness. They learn to evaluate good and poor living procedures in terms of consequences to all, and so to think in terms of the common good. They learn, in other words, to respect the authority of the *needs* inherent in the situation, needs democratically agreed on and evaluated with reference to their effects on others. They learn the meaning of accepting responsibility for themselves, versus the conception many pupils learn, that it's the teacher's responsibility to keep pupils from transgressing rules if he can. They help to plan the school work, to decide what is important to do and how to organize to get it done effectively, so they can think of it as entered upon jointly and after two-way planning, not simply as imposed from above. They read different books and exchange ideas (as against all slavishly reading the same). They learn to discuss matters of common interest with the teachers—school work, hobbies, life outside—so that two-way thinking, exchange of ideas, absence of group barriers become their expectation.

In contrast to regimes where teachers take entire charge, pupils here carry responsibility and learn by doing it to organize, to carry through. Pupils take charge of distribution of morning milk (checking on needs, delivering, collecting money). In some schools they manage the store which handles school supplies. In one school the fifth grade takes major responsibility for the library (checking books, lending them out, shelving, some cataloguing, management of collections of slides, pictures, and so on). In one school in an extremely underprivileged neighborhood a group of pupils handled all the war-stamp sales, which the teachers had previously managed; they sold an unusually large amount without losing a penny. Another group in the same elementary school took responsibility, with the teacher's guidance, for all the projectors, films, slides (caring for them, moving them to rooms where they were needed, operating, repairing films, etc.). They did it with thoroughly satisfying results and loved doing it, and their dignity in accepting responsibility, their sense of importance and self-confidence as they discussed the ramifications of their task, were impressive.

Pupils who discharge such responsibilities are learning to be responsible citizens, to meet obligations, to face problems themselves and to work out the solutions. They are building strength of character, ability to carry through enterprises, to persist in the face of difficulty. They are learning self-confidence and self-respect and to deserve the respect of others. They are learning to co-operate in working together for the common good. They are learning the techniques necessary if they are to control their own destiny.

What part does the teacher play? To summarize briefly, he helps the pupils to learn these things in the situations and framework of their own group living. He strives for and fosters the kind of life together to call out good individual and group living. He helps where he can to make things go well. When a problem arises, he helps them to face it. But he does not take responsibility out of their hands, for one of his primary aims is for them to learn to carry on their own living processes thoughtfully and effectively. As different situations call out different values, he helps the pupils to become conscious of what is involved, to digest and to think through the meanings; he helps them not merely to act on their own responsibility but to recognize that taking responsibility is involved and to learn, by doing it, that it is rewarding; he helps them not merely to have their own opinions but that to have one's own *considered* opinion is the mark of a real person; he helps them not merely to persevere but also to recognize that perseverance is a trait to be valued and cultivated for what it adds to the quality of life. The teacher, further, helps to extend the pupil's conceptions: In one situation respect for persons meant giving that boy a chance to express his point of view; it is also involved in listening to a parent's point of view, in treating minority groups fairly and taking into account their point of view—in this community incident on free speech—in working for the conditions that allow freedom from want. The teacher works, then, to make the pupils more surely aware of the conception, to think it through, to evaluate it, and so to build an enlarged and criticized conception instead of a blind or narrow one, a conception which they accept or reject after consideration rather than mechanically.

Instructional Practices Which Build Mechanization or the Reverse. Instructional procedures, too, may build regimented minds and so quite the opposite of ability to control one's own destiny. Practices which encourage memorization and verbalization and little more do exactly this. To make a practice of assigning six pages in a text and tomorrow quizzing in some detail on what the book said is to put a premium on memorization. (Some teachers wish the author's words reproduced as exactly as possible.) In so far as the pupils accept the ideas without thinking them through, they are forming the habit of swallowing what others think. They are learning to accept ideas handed down to them, by author or teacher, to take what is given and ask no questions. Frequently the recitation becomes—even worse—mere verbalization, saying what the book said without really grasping the meaning. When mere giving back is required, with no stress on understanding, seeing significance, using the materials to think with, the pupil is becoming an automaton, repeating what is meaningless in order to satisfy a requirement which was also meaningless. (If there is doubt that this is true, ask the pupil to put the thought into his own words, to use it in another situation, and see what happens.) Perhaps the worst effect of all is to accept that this meaningless reproduction is a satisfactory procedure. What more undemocratic and less spiritual way of living could there be!

Again, take the practice of learning from one textbook only. In so far as this is his only access to materials, the pupil comes to accept that *the* answer is there, that American history, for example, is in one book which he is now mastering, that the author's views are the only views; he fails to learn the important skills of looking at several books, of perhaps even finding his own, of choosing what is relevant from different books, of weighing opposing views. Instead he merely takes his own text from his desk, opens to the assigned page, and learns what it says. What a travesty on preparation in critical-mindedness, skill in searching out information relevant to his welfare!

To look at still another strand of this procedure, consider who asks the questions. It is possible to go into countless classrooms and listen in vain for an indication of pupil questioning or pupil curiosity or pupil observation. Whatever questions and proffered observations there are come from the teacher—his attempt to prod the pupils into participation, to see whether they have mastered what he assigned.

To get these ways of learning into proper perspective, the reader is asked to consider how perfectly they fit into the mind-building process appropriate for a dictatorship way of life—the Nazi, for example. Dictatorship wants minds which accept learning (and living) as taking the ideas handed down to them, of reading the books chosen for them, of asking no questions, of mastering details, doing the routine mechanically and well without looking beyond for its wider significance. Dictatorship, then, would find these ways of learning perfectly suited to its ends. For democracy they are almost perfectly unsuitable; as ways of getting and holding ideas they teach almost nothing suited to democracy, nothing suited to spiritual living.

For what is built in the pupil as a result of such procedures? Does he grow into the sort of individual whom others respect as an individual, with ideas and values of his own, thought through, examined, readily put to use, an individual with dignity as a person? Does he grow in ability to think for himself, in development of his own mind? Does he grow in self-directiveness? Does he grow in ability to control his own destiny? Does he grow in ability to be creative, does he enjoy the thrilling experience of working out for himself something important and satisfying to him? These questions are, of course, merely rhetorical, for the answer is obvious.

Compare, on the other hand, the seventh-grade pupils the writer saw beginning a study of the Middle Ages. They had read around in their classroom library enough to see the general pattern of the period and now planned how they might work together to study the period more thoroughly and inclusively. Each chose an aspect of special interest to him, but care was taken to see that all important aspects were covered. The teacher helped, but the pupils took major responsibility for the planning. Resources of the school library and also of various libraries in the vicinity were to be utilized. Each contributed proposals, each made a plan meaningful to him. Later as they came together for discussions of what they had found— each with his own card bibliography—they pooled findings and evaluated. They pointed out respects in which their own work was inadequate. All listened, all made suggestions growing out of their study, criticized, evaluated, and took stock of the further needs of the group enterprise. Plainly they were growing in ideas, meanings, conceptions. Plainly they had not spared themselves work or difficulty—several had used specialized graduate collections in a university library, all had delved more or less into what are commonly considered adult materials. That their processes of study were "communicating eagerness" to them was evident. No one who saw them could doubt they were also growing in ability to find materials for themselves, to select intelligently, to plan co-operatively, to meet difficulties, to take responsibilities, to stick to their tasks on their own initiative; they were growing in moral fiber. They were, in short, growing in the techniques and abilities of free persons.

School Practices Which Affect Integrity of Thought and Action. One of the spiritual values most commonly agreed upon is integrity. But though there is common agreement as to its desirability, are school practices of the sort to build it? Some schools give actual and direct moral instruction, some much, some little. A few schools state frankly, and by practice exemplify, their belief that its business is to teach subjects and that moral integrity is the responsibility of home and church. By far the majority, however, accept that building honest people is one of their responsibilities and take account of it to the extent of upholding honest and penalizing dishonest behavior.

It is still true, however, that in too many schools attention is centered chiefly on overt and flagrant violations of moral codes (cheating, lying, stealing) rather than on building the inner integrity, the inner feelings and desires and choices which give authenticity to overt action. What school practices will help to bring both inner integrity and overt moral behavior?

Some schools, as indicated, give classes in moral instruction. For young children this is a doubtful approach, for it is unrealistic to expect the young child to grasp abstract principles and—equally difficult—to translate them himself into meaning for the situations he faces. A much more effective approach is to utilize the situations of his own life to help him to take account of the effects of his behavior and to feel that it is important to do so. For older pupils the question is somewhat different though not entirely so. Experiences in their own living are still the ones most strategic for value building. Older children can, however, more fruitfully talk about conceptions and principles, but even here dangers are involved if the talking is done apart from actual situations. A real danger of merely talking *about* morals or learning rules for moral behavior (as over against actual moral behavior in actual situations being experienced) is that the individual may become accustomed to the verbalizing, that he may fail to discern that moral talk is different from and lacks much of being moral action, that he may become a divided self, a self lacking in *integrity*, one who talks on one basis and acts on another. The discussing, then, is best done when it helps to disclose actual lines of action and gets over into behavior as soon as possible. It should also be clearly recognized that moral action is the only effective test of moral outlook.

The studies of school children by Hartshorne and May[3] reinforce this view and add another dimension to be taken into account. They found that exhorting, moralizing, learning rules

[3] Hugh Hartshorne and Mark May, *Studies in Deceit* (New York: The Macmillan Company, 1928).

had almost no discernible effect in inducing honesty. They found likewise no positive correlation between honesty and going to Sunday school or participation in other character-forming organizations. What they did find to be effective was living (at home and at school) in association with those who hold high and consistently act on ideals of honest behavior and —perhaps even more important—living in an atmosphere which encourages honesty and, until standards and ideals are built, makes honesty easy. They found that pressures, on the home and in the school, which make honesty difficult take their toll. If the conception and terminology had been current at the time, they would in all likelihood have discussed their findings also in terms of what we now see to be inherent in their position, that a sense of inner security is essential to the building of honesty, of integrity. Without it, especially in those who have not had the proper experiences to build firm standards, the necessity frequently seems stronger on the side of dishonesty and lack of integrity.

Do schools provide an atmosphere which makes honesty easy for immature school-age youth? In schools where marks are the effectual criterion of success most children do not find such an atmosphere. Teachers giving or withholding approval on this basis, classmates reflecting in greater or less degree the official attitude, promotions which advertise to the world the child's success or lack of it and which allow or forbid the pupil to continue with the groups he knows—all these depend on marks. Parents too have been educated to see marks as the primary criterion of school success. The child's status, then, certainly in school and possibly also with his parents and friends, depends on his marks. In many schools marks are the criterion for participation in student government or other pupil activities. The child may be ever so eager to be friendly and helpful, ever so responsible, ever so anxious to do what is necessary for the welfare of the group, but none of these factors count importantly against the objective record of his marks. Isn't it asking a great deal of a child to expect him, when so much is at stake, to resist the temptation to cheat in order to improve his status? Olson[4] found it common for children with low marks to lose their report cards on the way home or even to erase and alter their marks. Drake, in a study of college students,[5] found they cheated according to their needs (to keep up the fraternity average, to meet social pressures). Younger pupils too, according to Hartshorne and May, cheat for the most part according to need. But the school sets up the conditions which call out the need.

Again, does the school situation encourage the pupil to be generous, fair, considerate toward his fellows—and to feel so in his heart!—or does the element of competition place a premium on the reverse? Only in a school where there is no competition, no comparing of one pupil with another, has the writer found children generally to be free and generous and fair in their praise of each other's work (secure enough to voice the approbation they feel, without jealousy or fear that it may react against them) and objective in receiving criticism and suggestions (secure enough to face the fact of imperfection without the fear that admitting it will react against them). It is common knowledge that schools set up a marking system in which only a few can achieve high marks and then give approval chiefly to those who do. Under such circumstances competition in academic matters is obviously the order of the day and those who beat their fellows receive acclaim. Recently the writer was discussing with a group of college students the effects of competition on those who fail. As these were students who customarily succeed, they could not at first see any of the adverse effects on the less successful group. Later, when

[4] Olson, W. C., Appraisal and School Marks from the Point of View of Growth and Individual Differences, in *Pupil Development and the Curriculum* (Ann Arbor, Mich.: Bureau of Educational Reference and Research, 1937), pp. 122-129.

[5] Charles A. Drake, "Why Students Cheat," in *Journal of Higher Education*, Vol. XII, November, 1941, pp. 418-420.

they began to see, they argued hotly that all life is based on competition, that it is a rule of life for the devil to take the hindmost, that they could not allow themselves to think of the ones who are pushed out. Is this attitude strange when their entire school experience has taught it to them?

Still further, does the school provide an atmosphere in which pupils build integrity in the sense of feeling it is right and proper to have their own thoughts, their own opinions, to say what they think, to be forthright? In how many schools are pupil ideas encouraged, accorded respect? In how many is it permissible to differ from the teacher? Among how many pupils is the school time a normal one to exchange ideas freely with others, knowing they need not dissemble or appear what they are not, that they can, on the contrary, use their own judgment, explain their position without recrimination? In how many schools, on the other hand, from kindergarten to graduate school, do pupils dissemble, say what they think is acceptable, give outward assent to ideals and standards they inwardly reject?

Or, to look at another area, in how many classes are pupils encouraged to arrive at their own tastes and values (increasingly criticized, examined, improved, but their own) versus accepting at least outwardly what others say is good. One high school class, given Emerson's essays to read, was asked by the teacher which ones they liked. No answer. "But you *must* have liked some," said the teacher. "They're classics." No answer, though some restless stirrings. "Well, if you don't like them, you just don't know what educated people like" This time various pupils began to raise hands and presently a number gave testimony. But to all appearances they were learning to say what was expected, what they didn't believe. It ought to be clear that there is a wide difference between the authoritarian practice of encouraging pupils to accept that a book is good because it is a classic or that an opinion is good because an expert (teacher or other) advances it, and the democratic and personality-upbuilding practice of encouraging the pupil to improve his tastes and judgment by reading good books, discussing what he and others see in them, and so building better standards of evaluation. Schools, and colleges as well, often fail to make this distinction and so fail to value and encourage the building of the pupil's own tastes and judgments above his acceptance of what "experts" say is good. The result is too large a number of high school pupils, and even college students, whose primary concern is to find out what the teacher expects them to say rather than to have a judgment of their own.

To summarize, for the building of integrity the child must have a situation in which he can live and accept integrity as good, as working out well—integrity of overt behavior and integrity of thought and choice. Essential to this are his sense of security in the situation and the encouragement the situation gives him, at least until his standards are firmly built, to act with integrity. When he has built really firm standards, adherence to them will become a factor in his appraisal of the good working of the situation. But as means to such ideals or standards the other aspects in growth of values must operate. He must be helped to get an increasingly clear conception of what it means to act with integrity, to evaluate its meaning for living, and to choose to behave so because he values the consequences to himself and to others. In integrity we have one of the clearest instances that acting without conscious evaluation and choice negates rather than exemplifies the value.

Effort has been made in this discussion to show how interrelated with school practice are spiritual effect on pupils and the building of pupil values. Nothing is clearer, in view of recent psychological study, than that intellectual development of pupils does not proceed apart from emotional effect, apart from the building of outlook on life, attitudes, standards, ideals, apart from the building of the quality of life which we call spiritual or the reverse. To take better account of these effects, to make our school practices consonant with the building of qualities which add to richness and satisfyingness of life for the individual and the group—this surely is the defensible approach to teaching.

Chapter VIII

SCHOOL PRACTICE AND SPIRITUAL VALUES—II

WHEN educators reject as philosophically unsound the imposition of values, it is their obligation to provide opportunity for value development by individuals and groups; and when educators reject as psychologically unsound the attempt to teach values through direct transmission, it is their obligation to provide opportunity for experiencing—learning value in response to life situations.

As already proposed, the reality of value content is in the response rather than within the material of the environment. The learning occurs as effort is expended to attain a goal which is meaningful to the learner. Thus painting a picture or cooking a meal may be experiences with value content for the individual, while breaking stones under compulsion in a prison yard has little such possibility. Of vital concern to the educator, therefore, is the provision of meaningful experience, rather than stone-breaking labor.

If the school program is built around a prearranged concept of content of the curriculum, the chances for value development are less than if it is designed to help children develop meanings. A program for value development requires the abandoning of rewards in terms of "stones cracked," which is the basis of much of our grading, ranking, and marking, in favor of respect for value developed. Evaluation of the school program must be in terms of experiences offered, in terms of opportunities for effort to achieve meaningful goals, in terms of responses made, values learned. Recognizing that the learning of values takes place in response situations, the program must provide children with opportunity to respond to experience, to make choices, to express themselves. This in no sense implies that merely the following of impulse is of itself a value. The value in learning to make wise choices lies within the control gained by the individual.

Obvious as this need for self-expression is, it is not difficult to find evidence that in many schools adequate provision is not made for it. In many schools a premium is placed on silence and conformity. Children must act according to rules which govern their slightest act, such as when they may be seated and where they may be seated. They are marched about the building in lines. They move from room to room on bell signals. In some classrooms they may be told when to open their books, which books they may open, and to what page they must turn. Little conscious provision for making choices is made. Neither individuals nor groups have opportunity for self-expression or self-direction.

In some schools opportunity for making choices is provided in but a superficial way. Participation in self-government may be a farce, and recognized as such by both students and faculty. There are student councils where it is recognized that a decision of the group will be honored only if it is the decision of the faculty adviser. In many schools, the only opportunity for group or individual expression is through an overworked use of the voting process. There is the well-known story of the teacher who asked for a class vote to determine which of two answers to an arithmetic problem was the correct one. As in any area of living, the form may not carry the spirit.

SELF-EXPRESSION THROUGH LIVING IN AN ELEMENTARY SCHOOL

Fortunately, there are schools of a different nature, where children are given careful guidance in the making of progressively more difficult choices, where their sphere of self-expression is enlarged and made more significant as maturity deve.ops. One such school is Highcrest, Wilmette, Illinois.[1]

The Staff Makes Choices. The atmosphere for making choices permeates the school living. It starts with staff planning. A few years ago a reorganization of the school district made it possible to form a primary unit out of a former rural unit. The teachers met with advisers from a neighboring university to discuss what makes life good for children. They decided that a curriculum developed in advance might not fit the needs of children. It was thought that the teacher who lives with a group of children was the logical one to discover what the basic needs of her group were, and that if she were prepared to teach she was also to be trusted with the construction and development of the curriculum.

In Highcrest today one may see children living in an environment created for children. The atmosphere of this school is one of informality, and the visitor can note immediately that the children have a sense of belonging there. They are at home.

Materials for Choice Are Provided. Each room has been furnished with individuality. Open bookshelves filled with attractive books and placed near a colorful rug make this spot inviting. Children may be seen gathered here as a group to plan, to visit, or to share stories. At times individual children may be found stretched out full length on this rug enjoying a good book or just relaxing. Maps, globes, and encyclopedias are conveniently placed to help the children add to their information and knowledge of the world. Ant palaces, aquariums, terrariums, and nature collections bring the physical world into the school environment. Children love to spend time just watching living and growing things.

Another part of the room is set up as a work center. Here

[1] This account of Highcrest School is based on a description by Mary Reese and Dorothy Oldendorf in *Mental Health in the Classroom*, Thirteenth Yearbook, Department of Supervisors and Directors of Instruction, N.E.A., 1940, Chapter IX, pp. 132-139.

one finds work benches with good tools and easels with fresh paints and brushes. Convenient shelves contain art media of many kinds. An oilcloth-covered table makes working with clay convenient. A ditto machine and primary typewriters aid in making creative writing purposeful. A small stage and several puppet stages encourage creative and dramatic pursuits. Rhythm sticks, drums, clappers, tonettes, psalteries, xylophones, bells, and other simple musical instruments give children an opportunity to experiment and to gain musical experience. A wide choice of materials facilitates opportunity for choice of activity.

Children Participate in Social Living. The care of the room is largely the responsibility of the children. Sweeping and cleaning and feeding the fish and animals are just a necessary part of the day's work. The staff knows and expects that children will make mistakes and have accidents. Children sense the feeling that perfection is not expected. A new boy in the school spilled a can of paint on the floor. He looked up startled to see if the teacher had noticed. A little boy near him said: "That's all right, you won't get the heck here. Just get some cloths and we will help you clean it up."

The children stay through the day. They eat lunch at 11:30 and then have a rest before an outdoor play period. The lunchroom affords many real jobs for the groups. They sign up for lunch and take the order to the cook. They set and clear the tables and do the serving. The environment is much like that of a good home where children are free from artificial incentives for learning, are not expected to meet adult standards of conduct, yet have opportunity to make choices appropriate to their maturity. The children initiate, plan, and carry out activities which they as individuals and groups have found both necessary and satisfying. Living in this environment, each child develops a feeling of security and a sense of belonging as he shares in the planning of each day's work. He senses that the choices he makes are important to the group as well as to himself.

Co-operative Planning. A day planned by teachers and pupils is vastly different and more effective in teaching values from one in which definite time is arbitrarily assigned by teachers for the learning of the three R's. In the Highcrest School the teacher and the group come together to discuss and to plan, not only the things which they wish to do, but also the things which need to be done in order that the group may operate happily and effectively. Children learn to make choices as a group as well as individually.

In the discussion of plans the teacher, as the more experienced member of the group, acts as a guide and counselor. It is she who co-ordinates the endeavor and leads the children into new and interesting activities. It is she who sees that opportunity and materials for making choices are provided and makes it possible for children to follow through on their plans. Children develop the ability to choose activities and plan well when they are provided with many opportunities to make real and genuine choices.

The stages in planning will be observed if we watch a first-grade group at work. This planning period provides one of the first opportunities for group thinking. A day planned by a six-year-old group might include the following activities:

> We want a work time.
> We will need time to clean up.
> We want a visiting time.
> We want to share stories.
> We want to write a thank-you note to Dick's mother.
> We need to finish painting the scenery for our play.
> We need to count our lunch money.

At the end of the day, plans are checked and the following day usually finds the group at work on some activities that had not been completed. The children grow in the ability to plan activities—for a week or sometimes, in the case of related activities, for even longer periods. The eight- and nine-year-old children demand continuity and hence require longer-term planning.

What Children Want to Know. Living with children in an informal atmosphere has given the teachers an unusual opportunity to discover what children really think about, how they feel about this world of which they find themselves a part, and the kind of choices which interest them and which they are capable of making. Educators have been so concerned about what children should learn that they have had little time to discover how they learn.

Questioning is a predominant characteristic of all children at Highcrest. The questions which children of ages five to nine ask show that they are intrigued by the unusual in their environment rather than the commonplace. They are interested in their environment as it applies to their problems, and the choices they make.

Value Development for the Individual as a Major Goal. In this school the goal is to preserve and develop the personality of each child. It is realized that no two children are alike. Each is the product of all the experiences he has had. Each has been subjected to socializing influences in the home; but the kind of pressures put upon each to bring about socialization has varied greatly. As a result each has built up a unique personality. The first concern of the teachers at Highcrest is to help each child find a place in the school society where he can live co-operatively with others and hence happily with himself, and understand values in group living as well as in integrity of self.

Jack and Bob are two first-grade boys at Highcrest. They were born in the same hospital an hour apart. They both come from homes that are above the average economically; both are mentally superior. Are they alike? Are they ready for the same school experiences? Are they capable of making the same type of choices? Jack is small, slender, black-eyed, and possesses almost perfect muscular co-ordination. Bob is large, sturdy, blue-eyed, and has a decided lack of muscular co-ordination. Jack walked and talked six months before Bob. He is the middle child of three boys aged eight, six, and three. He is independent, self-reliant, and eager for new experiences. Bob is the youngest of two children. His sister is in college. He is the only child in a house filled with adults. A grandmother and nurse feel that he is their special responsibility. Growing up in this over-solicitous adult environment has been hard for Bob. He is full of fears and uncertainties. He often says, "I don't know," "Should I do this?"

Knowing the background of these boys, the teacher helped plan experiences that would help each to grow in ability to make choices and develop values. Bob needed opportunity to do many things which were familiar and in which he could be successful. He was not ready for much group participation or for any organized reading experiences. By the end of the first year Jack was a happy leader in the group. Bob had found many things which he could do well. He had developed respect for his own ideas and was much less dependent on adult approval.

Jack was provided with new and varied experiences. He needed to use his energies to add to group living. As the boys participated in the school life each changed definitely. For a few months Bob would be independent and interested, then he would slip back into his old pattern. At one stage Jack was very silly; at another time, he was aloof; and still later, he was a sociable, responsible fellow. The teacher recognized these developments as passing phases of emerging personalities. They were neither "good" nor "bad" qualities to be fostered or eliminated by oversolicitous recognition. The boys were given recognition when it was due them, but they were not allowed to feel that they were objects of special concern at any time. They were given increased opportunity to make choices appropriate to the development of each, but if mistakes were made it was recognized that these were part of the learning process. Ability to make choices is *learned*. Values are *learned*.

The teacher's place in this type of program is not easy. It is she who must relate new information to the old in order that it will not consist of unrelated facts. She must give direction and meaning to information. She helps the child to make generalizations and to draw conclusions based upon his information and experiences. She helps him to judge the wisdom of choices he makes, and to see relationships. In other words, she helps him develop values.

When there is freedom of choice allowed to children, as in the situation described above, it does not follow that the teacher holds no values for children. On the contrary, it is her deep conviction that values must be learned through experiencing, which leads her to provide choice-making situations. She knows that although she may be able through various means to control behavior so that children follow the line which her values direct, unless there is freedom for choice within the situation the value is not learned. She knows that if the behavior of children is controlled by *her* values, that mode of behavior may be quickly abandoned when her guidance is lacking, while behavior based on values learned in experiencing will persist until replaced with other values. She is careful not to confuse behavior which is acquiescence to a prescribed pattern with behavior based on values held by individuals or groups.

SELF-EXPRESSION THROUGH LIVING IN THE SECONDARY SCHOOL

Turning now to the secondary school for examples of ways in which young people are helped to make choices and hence develop values, the educator immediately thinks of the role of guidance services and homerooms. These are important, it is true, but the main work of the schools takes place in regular classrooms, and it is there above all places that concern for growth in ability to direct one's actions, to make choices, to develop values should be found. We are indeed misguided if we believe we can relegate value development to fifteen minutes a day in a homeroom or a half-hour conference with a counselor once or twice a month. Development of ability to direct one's self and develop values must permeate the atmosphere of every classroom.

Planning What to Learn. In the following examples[2] young people are given an opportunity to develop values through practice in making choices.

For the past six years the boys of the Mont Pleasant High School, Schenectady, New York, have been electing work in home economics. When the principal, home economics supervisor, and home economics teachers first met to consider a program for boys, they soon concluded that a satisfactory course could not be planned without the help of the students themselves. As a result, the boys who were interested were invited by the principal to help consider the problem. With no books to guide them and with only a few magazines and some newspaper articles about boys' problems to supplement their own ideas, the boys and the teachers together planned this course. Each new group of boys has followed a similar procedure, using the outline of the previous class as a starting point, changing and adding to it to meet their particular needs.

During the current year, the boys started this course with a study of personal relations and social behavior. The work of the course was individualized, so that each boy received help at the points where he felt greatest need. Some boys, for example, wanted help on how to introduce people, etiquette at table, how to order in a restaurant, and the proprieties of conduct at dances. One boy aptly expressed his evaluation of

[2] The descriptions of practices in the Mont Pleasant High School of Schenectady, New York, Baker Junior High School of Denver, Colorado, and Parker High School, Chicago, Illinois, are based on reports in *Learning the Ways of Democracy*, Educational Policies Commission, N.E.A., 1940, Chapter III, pp. 140-141.

the course, "When you know how to act you can have more fun, because you don't have to think about how you act. You just do it naturally."

Later in the course there was a unit on foods. Members of the football squad planned their training diet. A group of boys and girls prepared food and entertainment for a supper dance. Many boys assisted in buying the food for their families. Then followed a unit on clothing, which included clothing selection, standards for judging fabrics, workmanship, and color harmony. Boys also learned how to take better care of their clothes, pressed suits, cleaned ties and hats, and laundered sweaters. Thus did a teacher show concern for the welfare of her students by enabling them to plan and carry out a course suited to their needs.

The importance for value development of the program described above was not primarily within the content of the course. Learning etiquette at table or how to press a suit cannot be claimed necessarily as significant content for values. But the fact that the boys had an opportunity to choose those activities for which they felt a need *is* claimed as content for value development.

It is true that some value content may be claimed for habits of cleanliness, social courtesy, health, and the like which these boys learned, but of major significance is the fact that they learned to make judgments regarding their conduct, which learning involves a skill more fundamental than mere aptitude in regulating certain segments of behavior. This skill, involving the making of choices about one's way of working and regulating conduct on the basis of such choices, is an example of value learning. We are accustomed to associate "value" with what we term "higher" or "spiritual" realms of living, but the processes involved in learning such values are similar to those in the homely example given above. To expect value learning in complex situations without first providing practice in the processes on such elementary levels is as unrealistic as to expect a student to learn calculus without first having had experience in manipulating the simpler number concepts of arithmetic.

Helping Children by Knowing Them. In the same sense, value development is an integral part of the program of the Baker Junior High School of Denver, Colorado. In this school, whose students come largely from homes of low income and varied national backgrounds, a teacher of shop has endeavored to fit the work of his course to the diverse conditions of his students. This teacher undertakes to visit the homes of all his students so that he may better understand the ways in which the shop course may aid in improving those homes. With this information about the home background of the boys as well as personal information about each, he is equipped to help them make appropriate choices and understand values. He then works out a program of shop activities with each boy and girl in the class. At the time of the staff visit, some students were cleaning clothes, some were pressing garments, some were blocking hats, while others were repairing and shining shoes. Boys were cutting hair, girls were washing each other's hair. Boys and girls were making toys, furniture, and household utensils of wood and metal. The show was indeed a demonstration of the education of "each according to his needs." Furthermore, it was a demonstration of how young people may be helped to understand needs and how to meet them. To the writers of this book, this process of discovering needs and choosing appropriate activities is the essence of developing "spiritual" values, even though the needs and activities may be as elementary as those described.

Moreover, the role of the teacher in value development is clearly illustrated in this example. The teacher played an important part in helping each youngster through first endeavoring to determine his needs. Thus it was possible for him to give assistance to the student through pointing out the contribution to living which might result from certain types of choices. This does not mean that a mode of behavior was imposed. Quite the contrary. But the teacher was in a position to help the student make judgments by being able to furnish ideas which the boy or girl could use in making choices.

SELF-EXPRESSION THROUGH LIVING IN COLLEGE

It is sometimes assumed that people of college age have the maturity to make choices unaided. That this is not necessarily true is demonstrated by the report of a college teacher.[3] His account of how mature people, teachers attending summer school, at first chose for consideration trivial, unimportant matters, then learned to choose for study those matters which were of importance to their professional growth, is a history of value development for the group.

The forty-two students enrolled for Education 303 were apparently not expecting a literal interpretation of the philosophy which presumably was to guide public-school practice in Alabama. At the first class meeting in response to the instructor's query, "Are there any questions about this course which concern you?" he heard such inquiries as these: "What is the text?" "May two students go together to buy the text?" "Are we expected to write a term paper?" "Will you give us our topics for a term paper early in the course so we won't be so rushed the last week?" "Can I get credit in Education 313 if I take this course?" "Will there be an examination and a term paper?" Clearly, some of these teachers with one to twenty years' experience were fearful of an ordeal. They wanted to know how much, in addition to the course fee, they will have to pay for the three credits, which they in turn would trade for a certificate or perchance final payment for a degree.

"Let's get acquainted," the instructor parried, "before we try to answer these questions. I understand that testing—evaluation is the broader term—begins the first day of school (some students are visibly worried) but in a different way perhaps than you have thought of before. It begins with purposes of students, what they would like or feel they

[3] This account was written by G. F. Stover, Professor of Education, Teachers College, Troy, Alabama, in *Leadership at Work*, Fifteenth Yearbook, Department of Supervisors and Directors of Instruction, N.E.A., 1943, Chapter II, pp. 44-46.

need to do, facing some problem that's really troublesome, or working out some plan that busy days in school have long delayed."

It soon became clear that these teachers had real problems. Some had hoped that they could find time in spite of course requirements "to carry on some study of our lunchroom problems," "to get some free materials badly needed." Few had dared to hope that work on such problems would constitute the course, that work on lunchroom problems could be justified under such a course title as "Teaching the Social Studies."

It appeared that some teachers had common problems, might even help each other more than the instructor could. So the groups were formed, leaders selected, responsibilities delegated, and energies released. At times the instructor was overwhelmed with requests for help. Occasionally some doubters asked, "Is this what you want me to do?" At other times the instructor seemed quite unnecessary as he visited one busy group after another, the situation was so well in hand, and group members were the experts telling how they handled "such a case last year."

If college instructors can successfully live through those terrifying moments when they seem to be the "least among those" at work on a problem, there will be ample reward in the unsolicited comments which usually come as the work proceeds. "I can really use what I'm making in the laboratory." "I'm convinced I can work this way with my juniors next year." But most rewarding of all will be the renewal of our faith—for frequently we have our doubts, it seems—that this vague thing called democracy can be experienced any time our faith in humans rises strong enough to release us from the "customary ways" to let us grow.

In this account we may again see the possibilities for value development through the *process* of self-expression, of making choices. The mature people of this group were helped to define their purposes, make judgments, and act accordingly—processes which are basic to the development of values, whether related to professional matters under discussion in a classroom or to problems of morality in matters of broad social concern.

PROCESS AND CONTENT OF EXPRESSION

In choosing the descriptions of practice cited so far, an attempt has been made to give emphasis to *process* as a basis of value development. The reader may feel that the situations in which these processes were operating were not those which offered rich content for value. It is true that certain situations may have more to offer in terms of such content, but the descriptions above were chosen deliberately to place emphasis on the possibilities for value development within what seem to be the most commonplace situations of daily living. Value development is continuous in living and takes place in all situations, for better or for worse. There are possibilities for self-expression in what may seem to be routine matters, and values grow through such self-expression even in experiences apparently barren of value content. It is the realization of this fundamental truth concerning the nature of value development which must lead us to examine the *total* school living of children.

There are, however, certain types of situations in which the content as well as the process may be richer than others in value-development possibilities. Even such situations are not of value of themselves, however. Even these are of value as the individuals experience responses which teach values.

An example of an experience which was rich in both content and process is the summer work camp of Fieldston School, New York.[4]

Twenty-four boys and girls of upper high school age along with five adults, we pitched our tents on a hilltop at the Hudson Guild Farm in New Jersey with the purpose of volunteering our services to the farm community. Hudson Guild is run by a settlement house in the "Hell's Kitchen" district of New York. To the farm come various groups from this underprivileged area—boys and girls for two weeks of holiday camping, whole families consisting of ten or a dozen Pats, Mikes, Patricias of assorted sizes, young men and women for their hard-earned days of respite from the heat of the city. The men are mostly truck drivers, longshoremen, policemen; the young women, factory and office workers. They

[4] As reported in *Americans All: Studies in Intercultural Education*, Fourteenth Yearbook, Department of Supervisors and Directors of Instruction, N.E.A., 1942, Chapter XXIII, pp. 288-289.

are predominantly Irish with a sprinkling of many other nationalities. Our own Work Camp group consisted almost altogether of upper middle class boys and girls of completely different cultural backgrounds, in addition to several refugees of German birth.

At first our group was regarded with a quizzical unbelief. It just didn't make sense—youngsters volunteering to work for someone else, and actually paying for the privilege! We were the "aliens" and the "foreigners" at the Farm—the outsiders with queer notions, to put it politely. But something happened all around after that first week-end, when our young people went into the hundred-year-old farmhouse they had promised to rehabilitate and started to clean it out, to rip down the old plaster, to shore up the sagging porch. Work spoke a language which words could not convey. That first week-end's work indicated that the group meant business; it bespoke friendliness and a desire to do the job and do it well. When, in addition, our girls helped to take care of the small children so that the mothers might really have a kind of holiday, that too contributed to the growing sense of trust. Work with the kitchen staff and the farmer meant new ties between people of utterly different background.

Presently, lines of communication were set up between the two groups, and as the summer flew by, they no longer regarded each other with puzzled suspicion, but became acquaintances and finally friends. There were baseball games and parties; there were mothers' teas; there were just the ordinary exchanges of neighborliness—a smile and a hello; there were flashes of insight and understanding.

In the illustrations above, the process of value development was applied in an area which may be said to have greater value content than some of the examples cited earlier. In this case the choices determined the relation of members of the group to their fellow men, but the processes involved were fundamentally the same as those used in choosing to learn simple etiquette and had been learned in frequent practice in making choices in less complex situations.

GUIDANCE IN MAKING CHOICES

In these examples an attempt has been made to give emphasis to the importance of value development through self-expression in the total school program. As said earlier, value development through self-expression, through learning to make choices, cannot be exclusively within the province of what is usually thought of as the guidance program. However, the guidance program may supplement in a significant manner the other aspects of the school program for value development, as illustrated in the following examples of practice.[5]

In the George School in Pennsylvania, individual guidance is a continuous process from entrance until graduation. On the daily schedule there is a forty-five-minute period designated as "period for consultation with teachers" and teachers are in their offices at this period. On the days of the staff visit, most of them were continuously engaged in conferences. If a student does not go voluntarily to see his adviser in the course of a month, the adviser takes the initiative and arranges an interview. Guidance is aided by a period of "diagnostic teaching," which occupies a large part of the first half of Grade X, the purpose of which is to gain as complete an understanding as possible of each student. A number of tests are given, and each student fills out a personal-history report. Teachers engaged in the diagnostic program meet every two weeks to discuss the individual students with whom they are working. At the end of the diagnostic period, each student sits down with his adviser and reviews his choice of courses. He may be advised to make other selections, but he is not required to change.

Upon entering the University High School in Oakland, California, each student is assigned to a permanent counselor, who proceeds to become acquainted with him as rapidly as possible. After the first interview, some tests are given. Then comes a talk about vocational plans, although no attempt is made to force a vocational choice at this time. As soon as the

[5] These descriptions are based on reports in *Learning the Ways of Democracy*, Educational Policies Commission, N.E.A., 1940, Chapter III, pp. 136-139.

counselor and student have come to know each other fairly well, one or both parents come to school with the student, and student, parents, and counselor together work out a tentative three-year educational plan. This is subject to later modifications, but gives the student something by which he may chart his course. All of the basic information about the student is kept in the hands of the counselor. The "core" classes serve the purposes of homerooms, and the teachers of these classes work with the counselors in advising the students, especially during the first year when the "core" deals with "Personal Management" and "Social Living." The fifteen counselors meet weekly under the chairmanship of the vice-principal in charge of guidance.

The courses in the Edison Technical High School in Rochester, New York, are highly specialized, and it is important that the boys have careful guidance in making their selections. Ninth-grade boys make the best possible tentative choices at the beginning of the year. During the year the staff seeks to assist each boy to discover whether he should continue in the field in which he has started or turn to another field. Several times during the year the boys are brought together in order that the general and technical phases of all departments of the school may be explained to them and also demonstrated by advanced students in the school. Near the end of the ninth grade each boy indicates which special line of work he would like to pursue for the next three years. At this time the question of job opportunities is also considered. It is possible for a boy to change his plans later, if a change seems advisable. Parents are consulted before the boys' choices are finally accepted.

In the University High School, Ann Harbor, Michigan, the guidance program centers in the homerooms. A student normally remains in the same homeroom throughout his six years in the school. Thus the teacher is able to become thoroughly acquainted with each student and to base his guidance on unusually complete information. The homeroom period is thirty minutes daily.

The homerooms are responsible for some of the most important extracurricular activities of the school, so the teacher has opportunity to observe his students in action in a variety of situations. The ninth- and tenth-grade homerooms, for example, manage the school fund drive, which is part of the community fund campaign. Another keeps in touch with shut-in children at the University Hospital, and makes all arrangements for the annual Christmas celebration given by the school for the hospital children.

The Phoenix, Arizona, Union High School gives as the first two purposes of homerooms:

1. To re-establish the pupil-teacher relationship too often lost because of the departmentalization of high school work.
2. To counsel and guide in educational, social, and civic matters, and as a means to this end, to discover and develop desirable tendencies and aptitudes and to gain a knowledge of the student's home life.

A well-planned homeroom program has been developed for each year of high school. Among the subjects included are orientation to the school, vocations, health, leisure-time activities, social behavior, and the like. The mother of one of the students in each homeroom serves as homeroom mother, and it is her responsibility to assist the teacher in maintaining contacts with the parents of students.

In each situation described above there is evidence of a conscious attempt to help students make judgments in relation to their way of living, the basic skill in value development. Enforcement of rules by a school authority might have produced, at least temporarily, behavior similar to that evidenced by the students in these schools, but training in value development would have been lacking.

MATURITY AND EXPRESSION

In schools such as those described above practice is given in
e making of *progressively more difficult choices*, in harmony
with the maturity of the children. No child is asked to make
choices beyond his capability to learn value in the response, but
every child is given opportunity to make choices, to respond
to self-urges, to learn through his responses. This is the school
in which values are learned.

To provide a school environment in which values may be
learned requires of educators that they examine the scope and
appropriateness of the opportunities for self-expression, for
making choices, which are offered to children. In the literature
of educational research there is frequent reference to the grade
placement of certain subject matter in relation to the needs,
interests, and capabilities of children of varying ages. Of
greater significance to value development is the understanding
of how to provide appropriate choices for various levels of
maturity. Little information is available in this latter area. A
major undertaking of those who would teach values is the
discovery of appropriate experiences in self-expression for children and young people, and investigation of how such experiences may be offered abundantly to enrich the program of
value development.

All which has been said here concerning value development
through self-expression is in relation to the total experiencing
of children. There are those who assume a division of experience with a concomitant division of the teaching function,
classing one area as "teaching" and another as "discipline";
one having to do with the academic content of the curriculum
and the other with the regulating of the social behavior of
children. If it be understood that the content of learning is
within responses of the learner, it must be recognized that no
such division of experience is defensible. It must be recognized
that values may be learned in response to any type of situation,

depending on the response made. Moreover, what has been said concerning opportunity for value development through self-expression applies to all areas of experience, to those which may be termed "discipline" as well as to those which may be called "curriculum." If one were to assume this artificial division, however, it is probably in the area of "discipline" that the gravest crimes against value development for children are committed. The requirement of blind obedience in major areas of living abrogates the principles of value development. On the other hand, value development implies a growing competence in self-discipline. To attempt to control deviation from conformity with imposition of restrictions to self-expression not only fails in its purpose but also denies the opportunity for developing values. Curfews for zoot-suiters in no wise mends the urge to hoodlum activity, and denies the boys a chance to develop values which might be made possible through experiences for more desirable types of self-expression.

It is recognized, of course, that certain types of social conformity are necessary to the welfare of the group, but the examination of school practices shows that often there are many which are totally irrelevant to the social situation. In other words, many of the standards of uniformity of behavior imposed in schools are not only meaningless and futile but, further, may impede the development of values by negating opportunity for self-expression.

Self-expression is interpreted by some to be a highly individual matter, an affair in which an individual communes with his soul, for the satisfaction of self. True, self-expression may take this form—the child who draws a picture and throws it in the fire; the girl who dances behind the closed door of her room; the man who sings in the bathtub. It is unfortunate, however, if thinking about self-expression excludes social implications and the possibility of expression through group activity. The value potentials inherent in respect for others, in unity of purpose, must be recognized by all who would teach values to children. It must be recognized that such values are taught only when there is opportunity for expression in group experiences. This aspect of the teaching of values will be discussed at greater length later in this chapter, but is mentioned here to point out its relation to expression. Learning of values through group experience takes place not merely by being in a group, but by expressing one's self in the group, and being a member of a group as it expresses itself.

THE ARTS AND EXPRESSION

Any discussion of self-expression must make mention of expression through the arts. But what are the arts? Watch the three-year-old as he ties his shoestring, creates a knot and bow. Could ever a master express himself more completely, on his maturity level? Could he gain more personal satisfaction, feel more truly his contribution to society? Are we capable, either philosophically or psychologically, of segregating the aesthetic experience *per se*? There may be those who claim this possibility, but even they will concede that the value development within self-expression need not be limited to expression through the arts. And even those who claim that no such segregation is possible, that the "art" within the experience is in the nature of the response rather than in the media employed, will concede that value development may be found in expression through the arts as well as in other areas. We will agree, then, that to provide ample opportunity for self-expression there must be experiences of wide variety, including the arts.

Even within the area of the arts, however, it must be recognized that *process* of self-expression is paramount to value development. Because an area of experience has been labeled "art" is no guarantee of the possibility for self-expression. There are schools, unfortunately, where "art" means filling in outlines with colored crayon according to a formula. Or some may consider it an "art" class in which the following incident can occur:[6]

. . . She liked to experiment with colors, putting bold blue and yellow and red strokes into different patterns on her paper. But one day when they were to draw a tree she had committed a terrible crime. She had painted the trunk blue, because she liked it with the brown earth she had made for the tree to grow from. The art teacher had held her drawing up for all the class to see and had said, "Dorothy thinks tree trunks are blue. What color should they be, Class?"

"Black," came a small and uncertain chorus.

"Of course! Don't you remember what I told you last week? I don't believe Dorothy even looked at the picture I put up on the bulletin board this morning. Some of you never pay attention! Or do you think you know better than the artist who painted the magazine cover, Dorothy?"

Whether or not this is labeled "art," obviously Dorothy's experience was no experience for value development through self-expression. It serves as a warning that the names we give to experiences are untrustworthy evidence of their possibilities for value development. On the other hand, the statement below[7] demonstrates the rich possibilities for value development in art experience when emphasis is placed on the process of self-expression.

When a child is at the painting easel in the yard, the teacher may show him how to wipe his brush or tack up the paper. She does not, however, tell him how to paint a tree or a house. She does not tell him what to paint nor does she ask him to name what he has painted. When he wants to tell about his picture she listens attentively. In no line of construction does she hint that he must make something. She realizes that manipulation and experimentation may be sufficient and that by "raising the level" of what he does she may be robbing him of a sense of having achieved. She never lets him know that his way is not worthy.

In the first few years of life many expectations are being leveled on

---

[6] From "This Little Pig—," Mary and Harry H. Giles, in *Educational Method*, Vol. XXI, No. 5, February, 1942, p. 236.

[7] From "Social Living in School," Betty Shuey, in *Mental Health in the Classroom*, Thirteenth Yearbook, Department of Supervisors and Directors of Instruction, N.E.A., 1941, Chapter VII, pp. 116-117.

most children. Children are continually being told what to do and what
not to do. This makes for dependence or for revolt, but never for a
true and deep realization of one's own capacity. Therefore at school we
place a minimum of demands on the child. And we stay mainly with
those demands which are important for his safety and health, and for
the health and safety of others. . . .

All demands made on the child must be demands which he can cope
with. Too high demands, which can only be acceded to with strain, defeat
him and make him feel inadequate.

In the matter of choosing which materials they will use, children need
free rein. They should not be told "Now it is time for clay," "Now it
is time for basket making." Choices which they can make and do make
day after day give them a sense of their own ability to choose goals and
work toward them. They grow in their own judgments.

This same freedom for expression of self may be found in
descriptions of art classes on the secondary level.[8] It is of
interest to note the implications that the processes for developing self-expression facilitate competency in the arts as well as
value development.

In the Parker High School, Chicago, Illinois, the art course
is characterized by regard for the individual talents and needs
of each student. The student may move about the classroom as
he chooses, now working with a congenial group of classmates,
now withdrawing to a corner where he can work without inter-
ruption on some project of his own. No attempt is made to
obtain conformity among the students in their choice of subject or materials. Rather, the individual desires of each student
are recognized and respected. The teacher strives to help each
individual in doing more effectively the tasks which he sets for
himself.

A visitor entering this classroom is likely to find five or six
boys and girls painting. Another group is at a table, planning
decorations for a school party. Two others are carving small

[8] These descriptions of practice are based on reports in *Learning the Ways
of Democracy*, Educational Policies Commission, N.E.A., 1940, Chapter III,
pp. 142-143.

panels in wood, while a larger group works on fashion design. Students are not competing with each other for some extrinsic reward or in order to see who can do the best work. Each is working on his own projects, seeking to express some idea which has peculiar significance for him. A bulletin board is used, not for the purpose of displaying the "best" work, but rather as a place where the product of one's work may be placed in order that it may be appreciated by all and at the same time criticized in a friendly and constructive fashion.

The teacher feels that respect for personality is impossible when all must work on the same subject, particularly if it is a subject which the teacher superimposes. His leadership is best exerted, he believes, in conferences with individual pupils, usually at the request of the students. The studio is always open, and students of all ages and levels of ability are welcomed, as long as there is room for them to work.

The art classroom at the George School, in Pennsylvania, is similar in many respects. Each student elects one subject in the field of fine arts (including music) during each year at the school. Students who choose art are allowed one month to "find themeslves." They work in small groups, and the two instructors move from group to group explaining the nature and techniques of the work and giving some time to each student. As soon as the student discovers the medium in which he wishes to work, the teacher helps him to map out a plan of projects suited to his interests. The staff visitor talked to one boy who was doing creditable work in clay modeling. "How long have you been modeling?" he asked. "I just began this week," replied the boy. "I've been trying to draw and paint, but I didn't do very well. The teacher suggested that I try modeling, gave me a start, and now I know what I want to do."

Students in this class have full responsibility for the care of all materials and equipment, a task which they perform quite informally but none the less efficiently. Last year, when they decided that they wanted to work in ceramics, they built a ceramics laboratory and pottery kiln with their own labor, donated after school hours.

"Tools" and Self-Expression. Perhaps there is no place in the school program where the principles of value development have been so cruelly abrogated as in the teaching of the so-called tool subjects. What are these tools if not for understanding and expressing? Reading, writing, and arithmetic may all be means to release of self. Each may be an art. Yet all too often they are taught in such a manner as to inhibit rather than release. Too often the phrase "language arts" is a snare which might better be termed "language drudgery." Too often the methods employed serve to teach children a hearty dislike of words and numbers, rather than the enjoyment of self-expression which media of art should bring.

For an account of how skills may be learned within a program for value development we turn again to Highcrest School, which was described earlier.[9]

Children are social beings and grow best in a social atmosphere where each has a chance to contribute according to his ability. Growth in academic skills need not hold a more important place then emotional, social, or physical growth. In the good school, for the good life, all aspects of living are coordinated and contribute to the development of values. Every child has within him the dynamic urge to grow, and it is the business of the school to provide an environment where without pressure, but with sympathy and understanding, he can follow his own growth pattern and develop those characteristics which make him acceptable to himself and to his group.

It is only in such an environment that skills can take their rightful place as useful and effective tools for better living. Skills need not be learned separately, apart from the daily life of the school. Instead, they can form an integral part of

[9] This description is based on the account by Mary Reese and Dorothy Oldendorf in *Mental Health in the Classroom,* to which reference has already been made.

the living that goes on each day. No group of children can grow together and carry out activities satisfying to all without finding a real need for the skills involved in writing, spelling, reading, and arithmetic. In such an environment children choose to learn skills for the need for skills is understood. Letters need to be written, happenings need to be recorded, and accounts must be kept. Learning to write or to spell is interesting if there is a purpose back of the act, e.g., contributing to the school newspaper or writing letters. An understanding of number concepts is essential before any drill on the fundamental processes can be of value. The teachers at Highcrest make use of as many everyday experiences with numbers as possible, e.g., keeping lunch orders and the actual handling of lunch money. The clock, and thus time and its value, is an important element in planning the day's work. Children want to learn to read and find a challenge in developing such an ability. Not all children learn to read at the same time, and in this school there have been several intelligent children who did not learn to read until they were eight years old. It is interesting to note that some of these were at all times definite leaders in their group.

Growth in any skill can come about in this natural functional way only when it takes its rightful place as a social rather than a mechanical development. There must be no pressure on teacher or pupil to accomplish a certain amount in a set period of time. Where teachers do not feel the necessity to attain certain standards of achievement in any set period of time, they think of children not as slow learners but as individuals who develop at different rates in different ways. You will find no dull or dull-acting children in such a school.

Thinking of children in this way eliminates the need for ability groupings. Children need to feel a likeness to their fellow workers. It is almost impossible to give them a faith in themselves if they are grouped according to ability, because children so quickly sense our lack of confidence in them. It is most unfair to give them a feeling of guilt for that over which they have no control. Children are not cruel in their estimation of the slower learner. However, they quickly reflect the attitude of the adult toward the learner and mimic the values of the adult. False values held by the adult, such as value placed on arbitrary standards, are easily learned by children. At Highcrest, children recognize that certain members of their group can read or spell much better than others and still others are more competent in working with numbers. They are willing to compliment each other on such achievements. But these academic achievements are no more important than making a good kite or giving useful suggestions in group discussions. Values are taught through the practice of placing value on successful living in the group rather than on standards imposed by the teacher.

The statements above may seem to dispose of the arts too summarily. There is no intent to belittle the significance of aesthetic experience. What is intended is to say that the aesthetic experience is within the response, as is the learning, and the value. It is to say to those who would provide opportunity for the learning of values: No program for teaching values is complete without rich opportunity for participating in the arts, but expression through the arts alone cannot furnish sufficient experience for value development for our children.

It is opportunity for expressing themselves, and through their expression finding themselves, that makes it possible for youngsters to develop values. It is our duty to offer every child wide, rich opportunity for such expression.

Chapter IX

AESTHETIC VALUES

THE AESTHETIC PHASE OF EXPERIENCE

THE aesthetic phase of an experience is the feeling of fullness, of perfection, of highest happiness that comes from contemplating a painting by Monet, from getting a complete insight into a principle of natural science, from building a birdhouse, from solving a mathematical problem, from cutting a figure eight on the ice, from completing a forward pass, from finding the girl of one's choice, from putting through a complicated business deal, from dancing to a band with excellent rhythm (or marching to a stirring military band), from listening to a Beethoven quartet, from buying an attractive dress, from decorating one's home tastefully, from reading a poem of Keats or a dialogue by Plato, or from doing a good deed. It is the feeling phase of experience that is realized when means and ends in an activity seem perfectly suited, and the subject of the experience, the person who is experiencing, is exhilarated.

But are these and an almost infinite number of other experiences that result in similar feelings, of equal potency with respect to the aesthetic response? They differ, but the difference in potency is conditioned by the degree of maturity and development of the individual person. Traditionally, the fine arts—architecture, painting, literature (belles-lettres, the novel, epic and lyric poetry, tragic and comic drama) and music—have been regarded as the proper sphere for aesthetics, perhaps because historically they represent the summit of man's achievement in this respect and have been set off as ideals for the most cultivated. In this class of experience, the art, the organization of means and ends, is more complex, and the act, either of production or contemplation, is self-sufficient; it has its beginning and end in itself, and it induces a mood of its own into the subject who is engaged in it. There is, for example, nothing external to a Beethoven quartet. It has no significance beyond itself any more than it is dependent upon aught outside itself. But through a most intricate pattern of sounds it absorbs the hearer into the exquisite perfection of its mood. It will have a like effect upon hearers who are prepared for it at any time or under any non-antagonistic circumstances, no matter what government they live under, or whether they are at war or are living in peace. Men recognize it as the beauty and the good they are seeking, and not as a means to any further end, or for any purpose at all save for its own.

The contemplation of the arts is not passive, but an experience—a positive response to color, line, rhythm, mood, and totality of form. The fine arts require a greater potentiality of response than do the simpler, practical arts, and it is by virtue of this that they have become separated from them in the minds of most people. Fine art is the higher because it has no purpose beyond itself. It is experience so intense, so whole, and so clear that it is a delight in itself. No matter how impressive and complicated a product of practical art may be, it has a more remote end to which it is bent and constrained. It does not stand alone. Its aesthetic value is therefore secondary to its practical value, the value attached to it by virtue of its accomplishing the purpose for which it was designed. In education, then, aesthetic experiences may be logically classified within two orders: those that delight because of themselves and those that delight incidentally. The line between the classes is crossed when an activity engaged in as a means to some external end becomes an end in itself, or conversely, when an activity acquires a purpose beyond itself. An instance of the former might be found when a student who has undertaken to read a great novel to understand better the times that brought forth the artist becomes engrossed in the novel itself; an instance of the converse, when a student of painting decides to use his talents as an interior decorator.

THE THREE STAGES OF AESTHETIC DEVELOPMENT

There seem to be three general stages in the child's aesthetic development. First is a period of undifferentiated aesthetic response, when any experience may be a thrilling affair—the dabbling in sounds, color, and social responses—without any understanding of its general significance. The happy expectant attitude of children as they explore all the elements of their surroundings without any practical purpose, and with complete disregard of their significance, is a pure, unmediated, aesthetic attitude. We do the child injustice when we attribute a purpose other than that of pure experiencing to these activities. If we smile at the romanticists who thought the child in his pensive moods was remembering heaven, we should be dismayed at the sentimentalism of the psychologist who thinks the child is consciously trying to make a practical adjustment. It is this pure interest in experience for its own sake that Dewey has called the "childlike" attitude, and in which he sees so much merit for learning.

The transition to the second stage of development takes place with the emergence of significance attaching to those previously purposeless responses. Some responses naturally result in pain, others with a moral bearing bring punishment; but most important of all, the child learns that he has power as an agent to bring about consequences. As this relation between acts and consequences dawns on him, he is aware of purpose, and may be aware of its correlate, responsibility. At the same time, the aesthetic or feeling phase of the experience becomes mediated, differentiated. His experiences bring pleasure in so far as his purposes are fulfilled, and frustration in so far as they are not realized. It is during this stage that the child enters the public school and engages in the planned activities of that institution. The second stage supersedes the first, but naturally the aesthetic content is not superseded unless through instructional perversion. Experiences may be practical or for pleasure, as one may play a game in order to return to a necessary task relaxed and refreshed, or merely for the pleasure of playing it. In the first case the game is a means to an end, in the second it is an end in itself. In both cases the pleasure may be the same, and one cannot differentiate between the aesthetic quality in either case. If, however, the "recreational" purpose of games is stressed, if one is told to play so that he can work better, or because he will be regarded as a good fellow, or because it is required, or because when he grows up he will make better business or professional contacts through skill in playing games, the aesthetic quality will probably be lost; in such cases we say the "pleasure has been taken out of it." This reaction does not so frequently occur because the emphasis in physical education today is largely on playing the game for the fun there is in it.

There are many instances of perversion, however. People who read books to "improve" themselves, and in order to be well informed if they are mentioned in social or business circles, those who attend musicales or art exhibitions because it is the thing to do, or who appear at "cultural" affairs to be seen, or who collect works of art to feed an egoistic sense of importance, are among those who have lost the childlike approach to experience that is the essence of its aesthetic quality. These are cases of arrested or thwarted development. Where they occur, it is indicated that the means and ends are not integrated in one unified experience, but that there is a purpose beyond it.

Arrested development may be caused in school when the practical is emphasized at the expense of the aesthetic. When art is regarded as skill in communication through words, painting, and music, for example, it is subordinated to something external to itself and is maintained on the level of a means. This tendency is the tendency of the new philistinism that sees social significance in all activities to the exclusion of beauty; it is an evangelical puritanism, the only spiritual interest of which is moral. Those with this point of view take upon themselves the responsibility of using all arts as techniques for ameliorative social organization—a very good purpose in its place, but unfortunate when it overrides the aesthetic development of children or adults.

The third stage is reached when the person is mature and cultivated sufficiently to feel the aesthetic experience as a mediated whole. In the first stage there is unmediated experience—just experience without apparent relation of means and ends except of the vaguest sort. In the second stage mediation takes place; means are differentiated from ends, and the relation between them is understood. But the stress is on the ends —on accomplishment, mastery of what is external to the experience itself. If development is not arrested at the second stage, means and ends become identified within a whole pattern, although the distinction between them is not lost. There is greater unity. The end is not beyond and outside of the means, nor is the means inferior to the end, but merely subordinated to it in the unified whole.

Aesthetics is not mere feeling, but feelings induced by insight into the perfect pattern of means and ends. The aesthetic response, then, requires cultivation. It is not an intellectual matter in the sense of being exclusively intellectual. It is an affair involving the intellect, desires, and emotions in such a perfect totality of pattern that the cultivated intellect does not appear to be important in the response, although it could not be achieved without intellectual insight. It is from this perfectly clear unity of means and ends, made possible by the act of insight, that the intense feeling of enjoyment arises.

Can practical arts give such satisfaction? Indeed they can, but the satisfaction is not so lasting or so bountifully recurrent.

The craftsman delights in making a perfect object, but the perfection of the object is measured by its success in fulfilling the purpose for which it was designed, not by the delight it gives. An airplane in flight is a beautiful thing. It has grace and smoothness; it is exquisite in design and a work of art. But it must fly and land with predictable precision so that passengers, mail, or cargo may be moved from one place to another. If it does not perform these functions perfectly, its beauty is of no consequence. Furthermore, when its period of usefulness is over, or even when it has become obsolescent, its beauty vanishes. A full-rigged ship was a beautiful thing when it sailed the seas, but was abandoned when its efficiency was lost in comparison with the steamship. It was the product of naval architects and master builders who took pride and joy in their work, but it had a practical purpose. The artist who paints the full-rigged ship, however, has no purpose beyond the painting and the delight the painting of the picture gives him and those who view it, and the pleasure is fresh for anyone who sees the picture as long as it is in existence.

ART AND MORALITY

The question may be asked, "Does not art have a moral purpose, and should not the work of art make a man better morally?" Fine art does not have a moral purpose expressly, for if it did, it would have an end beyond itself to which it is subordinated. If music, painting, literature, or drama stimulate licentiousness or immorality, or were created for the purpose of doing so, the particular art product is not fine art, because it was designed for an end beyond itself. Yet true works of art (and art will mean hereafter fine arts; the practical arts will be so designated) will be good in the moral sense. Art does not preach moral lessons, in other words, but moral lessons may be drawn from it. It would be absurd to hold that *Macbeth* was written to show the evils of murder and to serve as a deterrent to that crime. Although the playgoer is filled with horror and revulsion at the parricide (killing one's king is regarded as parricide), he is particularly impressed with the chain of acts and consequences that lead to Macbeth's undoing. If Macbeth were a monster, this would not be the case. It is because Macbeth is not a monster, but a man with some apparently outstanding virtues, a man not unlike the playgoer himself, that the latter is gripped. As Macbeth develops the common flaw of overreaching ambition, the play acquires universal significance for all men at all times. Everyone recognizes the flaw as one that he himself could have, and it is that recognition that fills the audience with horror. If anything, the play should lead to greater rather than to less self-control, but that is not its avowed purpose. It was not written to bring about moral improvement but to entertain, and it entertains by holding up the glass to human nature, showing to what terrible depths it can sink. It is art because the story is told with such perfection and plausibility and such perfect manipulation of the characters and plot that the course of action the play takes is inevitable.

Similar examples may be found in music and painting. Much great music (though not all) gives such a feel of exaltation, perfection, and power in its harmony that it has a positive moral effect. But that is not its primary purpose, its reason for being. Because of the harmony of movement, of means and ends, one feels more courageous, more balanced within himself (more temperate) and in his relations to others (more just). Music that is supposed explicitly to inspire virtue, the music of ameliorative and evangelical groups, does not appeal to those who have developed a taste for good music; some hymns are magnificent simply because they do not do this, but stand alone. Much popular music is poor because it is obviously made to "catch on" and is rather monotonous and totally devoid of development. But there are great classics in jazz; only the most arrant philistine could regard these as inspiring immorality. A primitive kind of music has as a matter of fact a sexual rhythm, but that in itself does not make it immoral any more than sex in itself is immoral.

Immorality is a perversion of what is good, or a deficiency of the good. Lewd pictures may be drawn for the purpose of inciting to lewdness, but these are certainly not works of art. Great paintings do not fall within this category at all. They catch the line, color, and rhythm of movement of the human body without seducing the mind; they immortalize on canvas the ideal of beauty of the human form, and in some cases, the magnificence of the human character. Portraits, or scenes with human figures in them, are acknowleleged to be superior to landscapes because they have greater meaning. Invariably the spirit is "lifted" by them. Cartoons that satirize human weakness, ignorance, vanity, are works of art in the same sense that comedies are, for comedies do the same thing in the theater. Political cartoons are practical, and inferior, in spite of the fact that they may be drawn to serve some perfectly good moral cause. They are calculated to stir up hatred or indignation against some person or group of persons. They are directed to some individual end external to themselves, and the likelihood of their having universal significance is small. They are means for arousing fear, or intemperate anger, and after they have served their immediate purpose, they have no general value. Satires of universal human feelings, however, are eternal, and make for better understanding and mental poise.

But although it is not its primary purpose, art does have a powerful influence upon moral character. Plato would have excluded the libidinous and perverted in art from his ideal state because he recognized the power of its influence for evil as he recognized the power of fine art for good.

But shall our superintendence go no further, and are the poets only to be required by us to express the image of the good in their works, on pain, if they do anything else, of expulsion from our State? Or is the same control to be extended to other artists, and are they also to be prohibited from exhibiting the opposite forms of vice and intemperance and meanness and indecency in sculpture and building and the other creative arts; and is he who cannot conform to this rule of ours to be prevented from practising his art in our State, lest the taste of our citizens be corrupted by him? We would not have our guardians grow up amid images of moral deformity, as in some noxious pasture, and there browse and feed upon many a baneful herb and flower day by day, little by little, until they silently gather a festering mass of corruption in their own soul. Let our artists rather be those who are gifted to discern the true nature of the beautiful and the graceful; then will our youth dwell in a land of health, amid fair sights and sounds, and receive the good in everything; and beauty, the effluence of fair works, shall flow into the eye and ear, like a health-giving breeze from a purer region and insensibly draw the soul from earliest years into likeness and sympathy with the beauty of reason.[1]

THE CURRICULUM FOR THE ELEMENTARY SCHOOL

Dewey criticizes the tendency to distinguish the fine arts as something beyond and superior to the practical arts because they are objects of pursuit by an esoteric, leisured few; but this does not mean that the distinction between them can be ignored. What Dewey is attacking is the attitude that deprives the practical arts of aesthetic value and would exclude the aesthetic experience from the lives of people in general who had little opportunity for contact with the fine arts. There is nothing in his writings that would identify the fine and practical arts without distinction; but this, unfortunately, has been overlooked by some of his interpreters. The aesthetic quality of practical experience should be exploited to its utmost, and the child should be given every opportunity to enjoy what might be called "pure" experience, a term used here simply for the purpose of distinction. The applied sciences are distinguished from the pure sciences on the same basis that practical art is distinguished from fine art, and in philosophy there is a similar distinction generally made between practical reason,

[1] *Republic*, Book III, Sec. 401. Trans. by Jowett.

or ethics, and pure reason, or metaphysics. Our concern here is with the spiritual, or aesthetic, values that reside in the experiences of the curriculum, whether they come under the guise of fine or practical arts, and the manner in which these values can be realized through instruction.

Although many substitutions must be made in the traditional curriculum, the solution of the problem of realizing aesthetic values in the curriculum does not necessarily mean glutting it with new materials or activities, but rather an examination of the materials and activities already to be found there, with an eye to shifting emphasis. This seems relatively simple, but simplicity in this matter is illusory because so much has been placed in the curriculum in accordance with so many purposes (some of which are more ill-considered than others) in recent years that there is no small amount of chaos. The organization of these purposes appears to be bi-polar in nature, some aggregating around the general aim of self-expression and others drawn toward social and practical uses. Because in practice these extremes have been nowhere as well integrated as in Dewey's philosophical statements, the aesthetic values have been underplayed, and the aesthetic quality has succumbed to such other factors as usefulness for social understanding and adjustment, citizenship, vocational preparation, health, tolerance, democracy, or some other end beyond the activity itself. Frequently the aesthetic phase of experience has been overlooked in favor of its usefulness for doing things children want to do without a very careful examination of why they want to do them. In the latter case, inquiry has not been carried into the nature of the child's purposes beyond those principles set forward by the psychologists, who, in turn, have limited themselves to descriptive principles, neglecting normative ones. As a result, the goal of self-expression, while recognized and sought after, seems to remain vague and disordered, for descriptive principles, as distinguished from normative ones, do not provide ordered purposefulness; they describe what happens, and why it happened in terms of the child's nervous structure, but do not relate it to the child's spiritual purposes.

When the child enters school, he is passing from the first to the second stage of aesthetic development, and his experiences, while growing in significance, or relatedness, have still clinging about them an aura of enthusiasm for activity for the pure joy of activity, whether it means anything or not. He likes musical sounds, not only because of the rhythm, but because the pattern or harmony is pleasing to him. Rhythm has been given an eminent place in education during the early years in order to develop the child's sense of rhythm further, because he likes it, because he expresses himself rhythmically, because it lays the foundation for healthful physical development. All these purposes are good, and all are meaningful, but the fact that he *likes* rhythm is the one that should attract our attention here. Herein lies the aesthetic value of the experience with rhythm. To delight him, the songs he learns need not deal with health, dietary matters, or social virtues. The meaningless chants children sing in their games when not enjoying specific educational supervision bear testimony to the truth of this. They love to sing and to listen to music for the sheer joy of it; that they enjoy it is enough. That socially useful knowledge and attitudes can be taught through music is just an additional advantage music has. It is well known that in the schools of ancient Greece the boy learned Homer by singing the *Iliad* and playing his own accompaniment on the lyre. He learned the virtues of the heroes he was expected to emulate and achieved the poise and grace that distinguished him as an Athenian citizen and a man of the world. But he also learned beauty through poetry and music and valued music for its own sake. Although the temptation is great to seek musical experiences for children through which they will learn something beyond a love of music—that is, to exploit the child's interest in music to achieve an end beyond the appreciation of music—the temptation should not succeed, as it has nearly done in some schools, where there is excessive interest in social ends, in stultifying the child's interest in music for its own sake.

The preparation of every teacher should eventually include learning to play at least the piano with reasonable competence, and public schools should be supplied with such instruments in order that every child may begin to acquire skill in the art of music. Appreciation of music is not passive; it is a controlled flow of positive energies and will be increased as the child acquires skill in creating music himself.

Because they are less expensive, the so-called arts and crafts have received more attention in the early grades than has music. The aesthetic values of these activities have been fairly well secured in the interest of "self-expression," and for the most part, the development of practical skill for the sake of turning out a perfect product has not been allowed to interfere with the sheer pleasure of making or doing that falls to the lot of the child under these circumstances. The greatest success of modern education in bringing out the aesthetic quality of experience lies, perhaps, in this sphere, and it shows promise of what can be accomplished in other fields. Much is done to make the classroom attractive, and there is usually a profusion of bright colors in generously scattered pictures. In an environment saturated with colorful art products, and in which the child has ample opportunity to exert himself creatively, the child's appreciation of art is measurably developed.

The situation is different in the field of reading. Reading is so eminently an essential for communication, the basic social art, that its aesthetic value is in danger of being slighted. It most certainly is a "tool" by which the child acquires knowledge of a social and scientific nature, but it is also an end in itself; it is within this latter aspect that the aesthetic value must be sought. There is considerable activity among children's writers to provide reading matter that will inform children of their social environment, health habits, and other useful facts and ideas concerning democracy and science. These are attractively designed and illustrated and serve an important purpose. And yet, although vastly superior, they are a bit too much in the tradition of the McGuffey *Readers*; they moralize in a more modern style and are means, rather than ends. Supplementary readers lean heavily on socially conscious descriptions of the lives of children in other lands and of other races (perhaps to develop tolerance). Straight stories with no axe to grind, whimsical stories about animals, children, and things that move in the child's environment, stories that are designed not primarily for information but for amusement, are the sort in which aesthetic values are really to be found. The usefulness of reading material presented to young children, however, does not affect unfavorably their appreciation of reading as a pleasure-giving art. If steps are taken to guide the child's reading so that he progressively masters the process, the mastery alone will provide the measure of pleasurable satisfaction necessary to prepare him to look for pleasure in reading as he matures.

The same seems to hold for number and science work in the primary grades. The activities at this level lead to application at a point beyond, so the functional approach is completely in order. The child has enough momentum of interest in almost anything to enjoy the activities involved, just so long as he can make progress, so long as he can complete patterns successfully. As a matter of fact, in number work, it appears that the aesthetic phase, seeing complete patterns, is immediately, at least, as stimulating to the child's interest as the use to which numbers can be put. In the primary grades the child is moving from the first to the second stage of development, from the undifferentiated aesthetic response to the stage where he is aware of the relation between his acts and their consequences. The meaning of things he may do becomes tremendously important, but it gets considerable impetus from the sheer pleasure of doing, from sheer activity for its own sake. The child has been given his start in purposeful activity, and as he progresses, care should be taken that he not be made to feel that all purpose is external to activity, that all activity, in other words, must lead to an end remote from itself. As he gets older—in the intermediate and junior high grades—it is important that the attitude he takes toward games and creative arts be generalized to his reading, arithmetic, and science activities so that when he passes into the third stage of development, which he reaches in the senior high school and in college, he will not carry with him the feeling that these arts are only tools, or instruments, and have no other value.

THE HIGH SCHOOL CURRICULUM

At the higher levels of education, the youth is acquiring the attitude of the mature, cultivated person toward work and toward all other activities of experience. He is learning to acquire knowledge and skill that will serve for immediate use and to lay the foundation for knowledge and skill that will be useful in the more remote future. At the same time, however, he is learning to enjoy the experience of relating means to ends in more and more complicated patterns; he is interested in the *unity* of experience and derives satisfaction from its unification. Furthermore, he takes pleasure in the *clarity* of the relations between means and ends in experience. In the third place, when the relations between means and ends are clear, and they are essentially unified in experience, experience is *intensified* and becomes more and more delightful for its own sake. What brings an experience to its highest aesthetic level, then, is its unity, clarity, and intensity. The little child naturally has such experience simply and immediately, but his experience has these qualities because it is so simple. As complexity succeeds simplicity, the qualities become achievements rather than data, or what is given. The older student is acquiring the art of unifying and clarifying experience and therefore of living it more intensely; it is a difficult art because experience is made up of so many varied and opposed elements; it is more difficult in proportion to the mature sensitivity of the student to the variety and opposition of these elements. Yet at this higher level of development the difference in the student's reactions from his reactions at the earlier levels are in degree, not in kind. There still remains the significance that emerged in the second stage, which, it will be remembered, was for end products beyond the immediate act. But there is now an additional internal significance, so to speak, that develops through the seeking of the end products in a clear, intense, and united experience.

Literature. In the fine arts, as mentioned earlier, the internal relations of means and ends, the internal purpose of the art activity, as experience is unified, intensified, and clarified, is readily recognized. Why should a high school youth read the *Rime of the Ancient Mariner*? Because of the moral at the end: "He prayeth best who loveth best All things both great and small"? Because it communicates useful information as a true account of a voyage around the Horn? Because it is necessary for the youth to know something about Coleridge as a man, and the poem gives insight into his life, his imagination, and his unfortunate habit? Because it is an expression of the romanticism of the time? Because it is a mine of examples of literary figures? Certainly none of these could be accounted the primary cause for its inclusion in the curriculum, although to observe some teachers approaching the poem one would think so.

The poem is a great one because it presents the experience of all men at all times in a universal manner. Who has not felt "Alone, alone, all, all, alone, Alone on a wide, wide sea"? All the loneliness in the world is in these lines. They *sound* lovely! Who has not experienced the sense of guilt for willful behavior, and the beautiful, exalted feeling of having done an unselfish, free, and personally disinterested act of charity? The albatross shot, and later the living creatures blessed unaware,

are excellent, detached symbols of guilt and magnanimity respectively. Moreover, in the poem, the experience is intensified. Man's hopes and fears, through the poet's skill in imagery, his use of sound and every poetic device for particularizing universal ideas and feelings, are felt more intensely than in the course of ordinary experience because the universal characteristics of human experience become clear. They are abstracted from the hurly-burly of everyday life, where the meaning of an event is not clear until after it has happened. The reader's experience is intense not only because it is clear but because it has unity; it is all of one piece. It wants nothing; there is nothing external to it that affects it and has not been taken into consideration. Although events are presented in chronological order, the poem is without chronology, for what happens is as much determined by what will happen later as by what has happened earlier; means and ends are welded together through the purpose of the whole. In ordinary life experience it is difficult to see meaning and purpose because one is so concerned with what is immediately present. Of course one has recollections of previous experience and can forecast possible eventualities, which, when he becomes attached to them, are purposes that direct his action. But the pattern is, except in rare instances, not very clear, the relations between the elements of the pattern are not always distinguishable, and because of numerous distractions of one sort or another a good deal is taken away from its intensity and fullness. Good literature does not have these defects; since it is concerned with basic problems of the human spirit in experience, it has meaning for everyone, and because it is a work of art, its meaning is worked out in a perfect pattern, clear and unified despite its internal complexity. The reader perceives the perfect pattern, discriminating the elements therein, noting that its effect is just right, that nothing could be added and nothing detracted, and that everything in the art product is perfectly suited to everything else.

The example used here is, of course, a classic, required in every high school English course. But there are many pieces of literature—poems, novels, and short stories—that because of their recent origin have not been raised to the dignity of the high school reading list. The writer's purpose is not to entrench classics at the expense of current literature but to show why the classics have value and to adjure teachers to bring out these values in teaching.

By the same methods that the classics have been distinguished as such, the teacher should be able to discriminate between the good and the mediocre in current literature and bring what is good before students for as intensive appreciational study as is devoted to the traditional classics. The fact is that the curriculum will develop more interest in many cases if modern potential classics are substituted for some of the lesser older ones where allusions to events contemporary with the author make for obscurity. But a work of literary art does not have aesthetic value because it is modern and timely. It must be timeless; it must be constructed in accordance with the principles sketched above, that is, it must intensify, clarify, and unify experience, and it must deal with fundamental problems of human nature in such a fashion that the reader identifies these problems with his own. They must deal with the conflict of human desires for love, fame, power, or glory with the rational desire for the good, the beautiful, and the true. They should show up the defects common to humanity, such as vanity, pride, ignorance, caprice, willfulness, and arrogance, so clearly that they are recognized for what they are, blemishes in all of us. They should show the effect of forces over which man has no control upon his reasoned plans and his desires. All of this need not appear, of course, in any one particular work. There are tragic, comic, satirical, naturalistic, realistic, and other types of literature. But they must *mean* something to the reader. The literary style, the ability of the writer to create images, to use words so that the sound is wedded to the mood and induces the same mood in the reader, his ability to inform the reader minutely concerning the time, place, and circumstances under which the action takes place as the plot unfolds, are necessary to the nature of an art product. It is through skillful manipulation of such literary devices that the artist secures his effects and produces the aesthetic response in his readers. Whether the teacher and students have selected a "classic" or a modern work of artistic merit for study, it should be selected because of its intrinsic aesthetic value, and the chief learning outcomes should be that the book or poem be cherished because of the delight the student takes in it.

Knowledge of literary techniques and rhetorical devices are basic to complete appreciation, as well as knowledge of the author and the time in which he lived, in other words, the sources of his inspiration. Such knowledge, though necessary, is ancillary to the main purpose of the reading and should never be permitted to overshadow it.

It may be asked whether books that are explicitly written to inform, persuade, or enlighten, such as biographies, histories, philosophies, or books dealing with the arts and sciences, and with current situations or politics, are to be excluded from consideration as examples of art. Some of these indeed have literary merit to a high degree, and the writers have considerable narrative skill. Yet they should not be confused with, or substituted for, works that are purely artistic. The principle of distinction lies in the fact that books of information or persuasion have an end beyond themselves. The writer is constrained to deal with certain facts, and if the end is to be served, the book must be subordinated to the end. A book on current politics in which the incidents were tinged with fiction would be worthless. If, however, the author has a journalistic eye and ear, if he can set down incidents exactly as they happen, and if he can make brilliant conclusions and commentaries, his book excels in its field, and an aesthetic response can be made to it by the student who enjoys the relation of means and ends in an organic whole. The student may perceive the meaning wrought into an immediately confusing situation by a synthesizing mind and a skillful technique. Yet the book, a brilliant one, is not to be substituted for a work that is completely self-dependent. It is not inferior or less worthy of consideration because it is not self-dependent; it is simply necessary for it to be distinguished from the works that are and whose chief value is aesthetic and not utilitarian.

Music and Art. Painting and music at the higher levels of education exemplify more simply and clearly than literature the function of art in highlighting experience. Music is generally regarded as the finest art because it is so completely self-contained. Schopenhauer says, in his discussion of the metaphysics of music:

. . . a symphony of Beethoven presents to us the greatest confusion which yet has the most perfect order at its foundation, the most vehement conflict, which is transformed the next moment into the most beautiful concord. It is *rerum concordia discors*, a true and perfect picture of the nature of the world which rolls on in the boundless maze of innumerable forms, and through constant destruction supports itself. But in this symphony all human passions and emotions also find utterance; joy, sorrow, love, hatred, terror, hope, etc., in innumerable degrees, yet all, as it were, only *in abstracto*, and without any particularisation; it is their mere form without the substance, like a spirit world without matter. Certainly we have a tendency to realize them while we listen, to clothe them in imagination with flesh and bones, and to see in them scenes of life and nature on every hand. Yet, taken generally, this is not required for their comprehension or enjoyment, but rather imparts to them a foreign and arbitrary addition: therefore it is better to apprehend them in their immediacy and purity.[2]

and later:

Thus, in general, music consists of a constant succession of more or less disquieting chords, *i.e.*, chords which excite longing, and more or

[2] Arthur Schopenhauer, *The World as Will and Idea*, translated by Haldane and Kemp (London: Kegan Paul, Trench, Trubner and Co., Ltd.), Vol. III, p. 235.

less quieting and satisfying chords; just as the life of the heart (the will) is a constant succession of greater or less disquietude through desire and aversion, and just as various degrees of relief. Accordingly the harmonious sequence of chords consists of the correct alternation of dissonance and consonance. A succession of merely consonant chords would be satiating, wearisome, and empty, like the languor produced by the satisfaction of all wishes. Therefore dissonances must be introduced, although they disquiet us and affect us almost painfully, but only in order to be resolved again in consonances with proper preparation. Indeed, in the whole of music there are really only two fundamental chords, the dissonant chord of the seventh and the consonant triad, to which all chords that occur can be referred. This just corresponds to the fact, that for the will there are at bottom only dissatisfaction and satisfaction, under however many forms they may present themselves. And as there are two general fundamental moods of the mind, serenity, or at least healthiness, and sadness, or even oppression, so music has two general keys, the major and the minor, which correspond to these, and it must always be in one of the two. But it is, in fact, very wonderful that there is a sign of pain which is neither physically painful nor yet conventional, but which nevertheless is suitable and unmistakeable; the minor.[3]

If Schopenhauer's interpretation is correct, a fine musical composition has complete meaning within itself, and the perception of this meaning within the complex pattern of sound and rhythm is an aesthetic perception. Youth should not listen to symphonies, string quartets, or sonatas because that is what cultivated people do, and therefore the school requires it, but because the teacher is trying to make the values of such listening explicit. He is trying to make them values that the youth will recognize and grasp once he has been introduced properly to the art. Fine musical composition is a development of an organic whole that does not depend on ideas, but upon the emotions, or as Schopenhauer puts it, the will. It makes clear the nature of desire and fulfillment through experience, as he has shown in the above quotations, to a degree of intensity seldom if ever realized in immediate experience. To enhance appreciation, or the higher valuation of music, there should be

[3] *Ibid.*, pp. 243-244.

instruction in music structure at the secondary level by teachers who have genuine musical training and understanding. Music should not be confined to large groups that engage in choral singing and orchestral performance. Provision should be made for the serious study of its basic nature in classes no larger than the traditionally academic classes in the high school.

The effect of pictorial art is similar to that of music. A painting is without chronology. The entire development of the painting, the purposing and fulfillment of purpose, are present in the painting that appears before the observer, and so far as it has meaning, as described in previous paragraphs, it stimulates aesthetic responses and therefore has aesthetic value. The painter uses his technical skill to secure harmony of color, happy distribution of light and shade, pleasing grouping, and a tone for the whole picture, but although this makes it enjoyable and gives pleasure, the effects of his skill are subordinate to the entire purpose, a unified representation of human experience in a clear and intense form. In so far as the student recognizes this experience as actually or potentially his own, the study of the painting is a success.

Science and Mathematics. The youth also enjoys other experiences that are aesthetic, although they may be in the curriculum because of their apparent immediate or ultimate usefulness; such are the experiences in the field of the exact sciences and mathematics. Let us take an example first, and analyze it later.

The child in the elementary school knows that the earth and other planets revolve about the sun. It has been demonstrated to him through the use of ingenious models, and he accepts it unquestioningly, even though his immediate observation assures him that the sun rises in the east every morning and sets in the west every evening, and both his senses and his common sense shout that the sun must therefore revolve about the earth. One of the most thrilling and satisfying experiences in the history of the human mind was the discovery of the true relation of the earth to the heavenly bodies, and it is repeated every time a youth makes the discovery for himself. This discovery may well serve as an instance of the point under consideration. It is a peculiarly happy instance since it involves mathematics, physics, and astronomy, and the method of discovery depends more upon inference and reason than upon the simple observation that all too many teachers regard as the *ne plus ultra* of science.

I. Immediate observation shows many spots of light in the heavens.

    A. Some of these are fixed in their relation to other points of light and seem to move around the earth as if in a celestial sphere which moves from east to west. These are the fixed stars.

    B. Others, the sun, the moon, and the planets, do not appear to be fixed in the celestial sphere but to move independently of it.

        1. The sun and moon, however, are regular in their movements.

        2. The planets are irregular, and by the ancients were called "wanderers."

II. Using simple methods of observation, the ancient Egyptians and Chaldeans plotted the course of the sun and moon and planets with respect to the celestial sphere. They noted that:

    A. The moon rotates in the direction of the celestial sphere of fixed stars, but it lags 50 minutes farther behind this rotation each day. At the end of the month, the moon has completed a great circle about the sky, and the celestial sphere has gained one entire rotation on it.

    B. The sun also rotates in the direction of the celestial sphere, but it lags 4 minutes behind this rotation each day. At the end of a year the sun has completed its

> great circle about the sky and the celestial sphere has
> gained one entire rotation on it.

C. The planets, however, move from west to east, slow
up, stop, move for awhile from east to west, slow
up, stop, and then move again from west to east,
which seems to be their normal course.

III. Ptolemy offered an answer to the problem submitted by
these observations.

A. The earth is an unmoving sphere at the center of the
universe.

B. The sun, moon, and planets circle around the earth;
the fixed stars are in a sphere at the very outside,
and this rotates the most rapidly. Next in speed of
rotation come the planets, then the sun, and last
the moon.

C. The irregular, reverse motion of the planets is explained as follows: the planets, unlike the sun and
moon, which rotate about the earth regularly, make
two circular movements, one in a circle around the
earth and another, around a point on that great
circle. This point moves regularly around the earth
from west to east at a uniform rate. Since the planet
is revolving about it, it is now clear why the planet,
in its movement, appears to slow up, stop, and then
for a period to move backward.

IV. This excellent explanation held from the second to the
sixteenth century when it was challenged by Copernicus,
who offered a more complete explanation, and one that
was in closer harmony with observations.

A. The earth is not the center of the universe. With the
planets, it rotates around the sun, therefore the irregular movements of the planets are not really
irregular, but only apparently so, owing to the fact
that the earth itself is in motion.

B. It is not, therefore, necessary to assume either two

circular motions in a planet or a hypothetical point about which planets revolve.

C. With the later discoveries of Galileo, Kepler, and Newton, the effectiveness of this theory was widened. All subsequent discoveries agreed with the relatively simple pattern that Copernicus had established.

The student who follows this reasoning through well-directed study gets a magnificent insight not only into the nature of the universe but into the synthetic, or creative (if the word is preferred), nature of the human mind. As he observes the facts, sees the problem take on definition, notes the emergence of the Ptolemaic hypothesis with its difficulties, and finally the Copernican solution in all of its beautiful simplicity, he re-experiences the desire of astronomers and other scientists through the ages for fulfillment, for completion and simple unity, and he thrills with the exalted feeling of realization that it is his privilege to share with them. Whether the experience has any value beyond itself or not is, for present purposes, of no importance. Such an experience rises above extrinsic value, for it is complete and sufficient unto itself. In it, man's struggle to relate the things he observes around him into a comprehensible unity is intensified, and the struggle of every person to unite the seemingly disparate elements of his own life into a symmetrical whole is made clear.

This can be true of any experience in the sciences and in mathematics to which a student may be introduced. Even though these subjects are studied for their usefulness, for a value they may have in helping the youth to realize his purposes in the future, they have tremendous intrinsic merit in so far as they are filled with opportunities for him to bring elements together into inclusive and simple patterns. His spiritual response to such experience is genuinely aesthetic; it gives him the feeling of exaltation and satisfaction characteristic of the aesthetic response. It seems that the teacher should understand this to be no secondary objective in these fields. It is not the usefulness of school experiences that makes them "vital," but the satisfaction they afford through realizing the youth's desire for fulfillment.

This argument may be reinforced from observation of adults who enjoy their work, particularly those in the professions, management, or the skilled trades. Although they are engaged in work that makes a social contribution, the social usefulness of the work is neither the source of inspiration nor the source of satisfaction. The inspiration is the problem, with the difficulties involved in relating means to ends, and the satisfaction is the successful solution through manipulation of skills, knowledge, and materials within the limits set by the nature of the task itself. The particularly successful operator is usually said to have done an "artistic" job when his accomplishment is perfect and when his attitude throughout has been keen. The designation "artistic" is more than merely a figure of speech. It is a fairly precise characterization, not only of the job done but of the attitude of the doer while engaged in it. He has enjoyed an aesthetic experience and, even though the experience was a means to an end beyond itself, he cherishes and values it because of the spiritual satisfaction derived from it. An activity need not fall into the category of the fine arts as defined earlier in this chapter for the "artist" to enjoy the pleasure of aesthetic creation.

CONCLUSION

All truly educative experiences have genuine aesthetic values implicit in them. When teaching is confused or dull, these values atrophy and are lost. The teacher who is enthusiastic (filled with the spirit) about activities he is sharing with the students gives learning experiences unity, clarity, and intensty. In so far as he does this, not only does his teaching become an art, not only does it become an end in itself rather than merely a means to the student's development, but the act of learning shares the same inspiration, and the student's experience takes on an aesthetic quality. One of the most significant achievements of modern educational practice has been the recognition of the capacity for enjoyment with which children are endowed, and the organization of educational experiences so that the capacity can be realized through totality of response within such experiences. Still, as it is hoped this chapter may indicate, the curriculum has tremendous reservoirs yet to be tapped.

Chapter X

SCHOOL ADMINISTRATION AND THE DEVELOPMENT OF SPIRITUAL VALUES

THE development of spiritual values in a school system depends vitally upon how the school system is administered. We hear much about observing the principle of respect for personality as the teacher deals with the pupil, but unless personality is respected in all of the relationships that make up a school system it cannot fully operate as between a teacher and a pupil. This brings to the fore a consideration of democracy in school administration.

DEMOCRACY AND SCHOOL ADMINISTRATION

Democracy in school administration is fundamentally a matter of the spirit rather than a matter of structural form. This is not to say that forms of organization are not important. Rather, the forms without the spirit are empty symbols or worse. A school superintendent who establishes an administrative council proclaiming it to be representative of the entire school corps and to have the function of democratically evolving objectives and policies for the administration of the school system should be determined to make it what is proclaimed for it. If he not only presides over the council himself but does so in such a way as to defeat the announced purpose, he is a much greater enemy of democracy in school administration than is another superintendent who makes no pretense of collaboration with his fellow workers. The latter is at least forthright, a trait in itself of high spiritual value, whereas the former is undermining the ideal that he professes to support.

A superintendent who does not intend that an administrative council shall make decisions unless they happen to coincide with his preconceived views is stultifying personality to a degree that is certain seriously to pervade the entire life of the school system. To the extent that a superintendent of schools is himself held finally responsible by the board of education for recommendations of policy and objectives, he cannot, of course, delegate this responsibility. He should make no pretense of doing so. The forthright thing is to state this fact clearly to his associates and to announce that their relationship to him in such matters, whether expressed through an administrative council or by any other means, is limited to the advisory function.

This by no means vitiates the function of an administrative council as much as it might seem. It depends on the spirit of the thing. If the superintendent thoroughly appreciates the implications of the democratic principle, he will see in it the most intelligent manner of arriving at decisions. It means that the strongest possible position available to him, as he goes to his board of education with an important recommendation, is one in which he is supported by all of the intelligence which can be derived from co-operative study by his professional associates and himself. If he thoroughly believes this, his associates will soon recognize the fact, and on the rare occasions when he might find it necessary to disagree with the consensus of his advisory group, such disagreement will not be resented.

A board of education which wants to perform the best possible service for its community will want its superintendent of schools to proceed along the lines which will enable him to come to the board with a maximum of intelligence back of his recommendations. This will frequently require that the base of discussion preliminary to recommendations be extended beyond the professional corps of the school system to include lay groups and students from the schools. Most boards will accept the thesis that the superintendent who formulates his recommendations in the light of the total thought contributions of all parties concerned is proceeding in the most constructive way possible. They may not think to call it democracy in school administration. It may be called just plain common sense.

The emphasis above given to the relationships of the superintendent to the school corps, the board of education, and the community at large is not intended to imply an undervaluation of the many areas of responsibility, the many and varied, more specific, human relationships involved in the everyday life of a school system. The reactions of teachers, principals, supervisors, superintendent, parents, pupils to one another are of the essence. All of these relationships reflect the spiritual values, or lack of them, in the persons involved and influence everyone for better or worse. With the question, "Am I fully respecting the other person?" uppermost in mind, there is a definite responsibility upon everyone to study himself with reference to his effect upon other people with whom he is associated. Not by any means does all responsibility for democracy in school life rest upon the administrator, but he is in a position of extraordinary advantage in working for it. It should be a primary aim of administrators to effect as much consistency as possible among all practices of the school system and the spiritual values which the schools are trying to develop.

Once this spirit of respect for personality comes to pervade a school system, it has definite practical implications that vitally affect the teacher and all associated with him. In fact, unless in the practical matters of school administration this spirit is manifest, it cannot be said that the principle of respect for personality has at best gone farther than the lip-service stage. "Don't say things. What you are stands over you the while, and thunders so that I cannot hear what you say to the contrary" was never more to the point than here.

As only one practical aspect of administration and solely for illustrative purposes, let us consider how this applies to the method by which teachers are paid their salaries. It should be kept in mind here that it is the question of "method" we are discussing, not amounts of salary *per se* or any factor that expresses the mercenary or selfish attitude. It is the "manner of treatment" reflected in the so-called practical aspects of administration that concerns us in a discussion of spiritual values.

From the point of view of respect for personality it is vital that salaries be paid teachers under the method of a schedule which reduces to the lowest minimum possible all subjective factors in determining the teacher's place on the schedule. Whether a teacher will get a small increment, a large increment, or no increment at all this year depends upon the subjective reaction of a principal, a supervisor, a superintendent, a school board committee, a school board, or all combined. To the extent this is the case, the teacher's personality is subordinated to another personality or personalities in a manner which, no matter how good the intentions, is likely to be more or less capricious. To appreciate the issue involved here, one has only to observe what happens to the morale of teachers in a school system in which, even though liberal salaries are paid and increments are granted every year, the teacher is made to feel that whether he gets an increment depends on how well he has conformed to the thinking of one or more supervising officials. Under such circumstances he is bound to suspect that at best an honest "difference of opinion" between him and a supervising official on some issue of education may interfere with the progress of his salary status. In this circumstance two courses are open to him. One is to leave the school system and the other is to conform in a manner contrary to his inner beliefs. The bad spiritual effects of the latter alternative call for no elucidation. His leaving the school system may solve the problem for him but not for the school system. In the long run a school system which forces this choice on a teacher of virile spirit will, though perhaps unconsciously, select teachers of the colorless, subservient type. A school system staffed by teachers selected under this principle can hardly provide the best situation for the development of creative, resourceful, vigorous personalities among its boys and girls.

THE METHOD OF SOCIAL CONTROL

This brief discussion of the method by which the awarding of salary increments is administered may seem to imply that order is to give way to chaos. Such a result would, of course, destroy all spiritual values. That any society must exercise control over itself is a truism. The only issue here concerns the method of social control as it operates through school administration. Those who argue that a teacher's yearly salary increments should depend on some person's judgment or the collective judgment of certain persons are in danger of seeming to want to use the awarding of salary increments as a method of social control. This is a dangerous device to apply to teachers in a democracy. Its chief danger lies in the implied presumption that there is a specific detailed authoritarian life pattern for the establishment and maintenance of which the administrative authorities are responsible. It is further presumed that they know how to measure in fine degree the extent to which the year's work of a particular teacher has contributed to the realization of the pattern. The arbitrary nature of such a method of control is generally felt with stultifying effect by those to whom it is applied.

In a democracy the best way of life cannot be wholly preconceived, wrapped up in a package, and handed to a teacher by his superiors to pass on to his pupils. The best is always emerging. It is never fully known. Control resides in the orderly procedure from the known to the unknown. Obviously, then, the social heritage cannot be ignored. No one will deny that the social heritage is of fundamental importance as a guiding factor. We will all stoutly maintain that every teacher should possess that degree of scholarship which guarantees that he will be familiar with the essentials of this heritage and that he should possess the discipline necessary to the intelligent use of it as a means of throwing light upon the path ahead. But it is this scholarship upon which we should rely for control of the process of growth in spiritual values. We cannot foretell in every particular where it will lead us but we can have unshakable faith in its being the best guide that we have. In fact, if we do not have this faith, we cannot claim to believe in the fundamentals of the democratic principle. It requires courage to rest our concern about the control and direction of education upon this principle, but here again we are getting right at the heart of democracy, the question of whether we believe in man. If we do not believe in this kind of control, then, *ipso facto*, we believe in some arbitrary form of control. We accept tyranny over the mind of man as right. Democracy, owing to the dynamic principle that characterizes it, is a venturesome business, but only the adventuresome life is worth while to the virile spirit.

Adventuresomeness is not recklessness. It is in a certain fundamental sense the very opposite, inasmuch as only to the degree that we constructively use our experience in shaping new life, life that we have never before seen, do we make our survival most certain.

There is nothing in adventuresomeness that disrespects experience. It is, in fact, the only value that makes a fully respectful place in our lives for experience. No situation in the world today, characterized to any appreciable degree by democratic living, was made that way by foisting upon the people a preconceived blueprint of living. The bold outlines of the democratic life we can clearly derive from our experience, but the specific ways of living tomorrow to which the free thought and free speech of today will lead us cannot be foreseen. We cannot intelligently accept this principle of life for our society at large and deny it to the inner life of our society's schools. The authors believe that the public schools have in recent decades made great progress in the practice of this principle and that by so doing they have made a contribution of the most fundamental sort to the spiritual values of our civilization. Progress in the practice of this principle is rapidly spreading in our public schools, and in its further development the fate of the spirit upon which our country was founded rests in high degree. The problem is to use our social heritage in such a way as to develop the spiritually strong person, one who makes use of the past as a means of guidance in going forward to a better future. Only thus can the spirit grow.

It should be clear, then, that social control in a democracy rests upon the individual's capacity for self-control and that the individual does not possess this capacity unless he is able wisely to proceed from the known to the unknown. It should also be clear that no person whose knowledge of experience pertinent to his growth is lacking possesses this capacity. This implies the necessity not only of scope of experience but of the integration of experience into a meaningful whole. Only thus can a novel situation be intelligently appraised by reference to the past. If one's familiarity with the past is fragmentary, disintegrated, he will be unable to relate experience effectively to his present problems. He will himself be disintegrated. To the extent that he lacks unity within himself is he weak and ineffective. "In unity there is strength" applies to things spiritual as well as to things physical. It is basic to order in a democracy.

THE STRUCTURAL SCHOOL OF LIFE

In the development of an integrated life for the individual, the structure of school life is of vital importance. The administrator should be continuously alert to ways by which this structure can be made more conducive to the development within the individual of a unified outlook upon life. The structure should be consonant with the idea of unity as opposed to disintegration. In this connection let us take special note of the following structure which even yet all too often characterizes our schools.

We first organize the subject matter that we wish to present by horizontal sections. In the typical school system the larger horizontal sections consist of a high school and an elementary school, or a senior high school, a junior high school, and an elementary school. Frequently the elementary school is conceived of as consisting of a kindergarten and then the elementary school. There generally is a marked cleavage between any two of these sections, but the tendency toward cleavage does not stop here. We divide the elementary school horizontally into yearly assignments of subject matter called grades. Likewise, we divide the junior high school and the senior high school. In some school systems these grades are divided horizontally into semesters or even smaller sections. Textbooks are adopted in accordance with these horizontal divisions. Pupils, teachers, and rooms are assigned in accordance with them to such a degree that going from the fourth grade to the fifth is, for example, considered to be a definite problem in adaptation. Teachers, courses of study, and textbook materials become highly specialized in terms of these divisions.

However, we are not at this point through with the problem of a disintegrative type of structure. After we have made the divisions above depicted on a horizontal basis, we divide subject matter into vertical sections. Such sections may be confined to one grade or they may extend through several grades. English, mathematics, social studies, for example, may represent vertical organization of subject matter extending through most of the pupil's school life. This type of division reaches its most extreme form in the high school years. In these years not only is subject matter divided by special fields but teachers are assigned according to them. Frequently this type of teacher assignment occurs also in the elementary grades but there it is the exception. In the high school it is the rule. This form of division is carried so far in high schools that it is not uncommon for the various subject-matter departments to be operating upon practically a mutually exclusive basis. One department does not know what the other is doing.

Thus we have a structure, if such it may be called, that by its nature presents division to the pupil from his earliest day in school. First, division by horizontal organizations of subject matter and teachers as above pointed out and then such division by vertical sections. Somehow we expect a pupil to put this altogether into a unified whole. By hearing one teacher pound on one key and another teacher on another, he is supposed to construct the keyboard. Thus we do the comparatively easy thing ourselves and leave to the pupil almost unaided the most difficult job in education.

Obviously the structure above depicted was not consciously created for the purpose of disintegrating the individual. No doubt the theory has been that efficient administration would so connect the high school with the elementary school, one grade with another, one subject-matter field with another, that the development of the individual would be properly integrated. In other words, the pupil would be conditioned to a preconceived, closely knit pattern. But experience surely is convincing to the effect that, quite aside from the fundamental error implied that unity in the individual can be effected through presentation of subject matter externally organized, this was too big an order upon devices and techniques of administration. Teachers' meetings and general discussions have not been sufficient. Many school systems have attempted to bridge the gaps by employing special personnel in guidance, personnel that is supposed to see the picture whole and help the pupil thus to see it. The authors of this Yearbook would in no sense decry the employment of personnel that is to give continuous special attention to the problem of guidance, provided it does not represent an antidote to ingredients that should never have been introduced. In other words, to build up on the one hand a structure which in itself causes disintegration and then set up on the other a structure that is supposed to overcome disintegration could hardly commend itself to the intelligence. It would be far more constructive to build in the first place in terms of the unified, integrated growth of the pupil.

The authors are not unaware of the fact that many school systems have made progress toward this end and that some have made a great deal of progress. Elementary school life in many cases is being organized in larger units, each of which may cover several years of a pupil's life, with formal subject-matter lines subordinated to the growth of the pupil. Gradually the organization of elementary schools in terms of formal subject matter by grades or classes is giving way to procedures directed by consideration of the growth needs of pupils. Many efforts are under way to break down compartmentalization in the high schools in order that the needs of the pupil to grasp life whole may be better served. These tendencies need to be carried to a point which enables us to see that the administrative structure of our schools in itself offers no artificial barriers to the development of the integrated life.

This is not to say that areas of special knowledge are to be ignored. We must have our specialists in the various fields of knowledge. Special knowledge is essential to progress in the whole of which it is a part, but we must, as a primary consideration in education, have a corps of teachers and administrators who are responsible for seeing the whole problem of life with the pupil. It is the function of this corps to go forward with the pupil from his earliest day in school, drawing from the various special fields of knowledge as the needs of the pupil may dictate. The various fields of special knowledge will not, in the training and experience of any one teacher, be available in sufficient degree to carry this process out. We must have persons in our school corps who embody the special fields of knowledge, persons to whom we can look for scholarly teaching with respect to any one of these fields. But we cannot leave to them alone the fundamental responsibility of guidance nor can we meet our responsibility with regard to this function by stepping into the pitfall of overspecialization from another angle, namely, that of merely having available specialists in guidance operating outside of the center of the educational stream. Centering in the leadership of a teacher of a group in which the teacher is the general practitioner of education, the educational process should reach out to the special fields and should derive from each of them what is most pertinent to the life of the individual pupil. The general-practitioner-of-education-teacher should be supported by an administrative policy which makes available to him such variety of special helps from highly qualified specialists as may be pertinent to the well-rounded development of the individual.

THE TEACHER AS A PROFESSIONAL PRACTITIONER

The teacher must be fully conscious of himself as an individual member of a great profession. The mere fact that we find it necessary to hold school in buildings, a large number of pupils and many teachers under one roof, presents pitfalls before the realization of this value. Such a gathering suggests organization. Our traditional technique of organization in such a situation is to put one person in charge. This means in an individual school a principal in charge of the teachers, in a school system a superintendent in charge. The line of least resistance in making this operate in an orderly manner is the undue subordination of personality all along the line.

Nothing is here intended by way of argument against organization as such. Organization there must be unless we believe in chaos. The whole point is, "What kind of organization?" On the premise of a thoroughly scholarly teacher, the point is that in a democracy efficient organization will be directed toward freeing the teacher to act, restricted only by his intelligence.

If this seems like a suggestion of anarchy let us consider this premise of a scholarly teacher and of intelligence as the unifying principle. Intelligence never carries the unique to the point of chaos. But there is a fundamental difference between arriving at co-operation and unity by the free road and arriving at it by the false unity effected through suppression and acquiescence. The free road leads to such unity as intelligence commends as a basis for the highest type of individual life, the life in which the individual is free to create, to improve, to move higher into the realm of spiritual values.

This discussion by no means, then, resolves itself into an argument for no structure at all, for no organization at all in school life. This would be most absurd. Rather the suggestion is that we undertake the hardest job known in planning and organization—organizing and planning for respect for personality in our school life.

The importance here ascribed to the teacher requires that degree of social sanction which will make teaching satisfactory to the ablest people as a lifetime career. That situation in which a teacher must look to appointment to a supervisorship, principalship, or superintendency as the way by which to acquire full respectability, economic or otherwise, simply does not belong in a democracy. We should be quick to see the stultifying effects upon the practice of medicine if the practitioner in the field, our "family physician," were made less than what he is, a person whom we could not respect, a person who could not respect himself unless and until he became a superintendent of a group of physicians. Something analogous to this respect for the individual practitioner of medicine is needed in the instance of the school teacher.

Under the principle of democracy in school administration it is incumbent upon the administrator to be creative. In recent decades we have had much discussion of the value of creativeness in the classroom, creativeness in the work of the teacher with pupils. This is all to the good and should not in any sense be neglected. But there perhaps has been too little discussion of the obligation that this places upon the administrator to be creative. Creativeness in the teacher-pupil relationship calls for the use of new procedures. Frequently when this is seen to be the case the teacher gets the answer from some administrator: "Yes, it's a good idea but it is impracticable." Sometimes, no doubt in spite of all the administrator can do, the idea does remain impracticable for the time being, but obviously it is the peculiar responsibility of the administrator to be effective in so reshaping the general situation as to make the new idea that seems good practicable, at least to the extent of giving it a trial. There is no absolute immutability to our holding school for just certain months in the year, for certain hours in the day, for the teaching of certain subjects just as we have known these subjects and as we have taught them, for keeping out of the school program many activities that promise good for the boys and girls and for society, for holding school altogether in school buildings as opposed to taking school life into the community, for beginning school experience at five or six years of age and ending at seventeen or eighteen, for organizing school life by the rigid pattern now represented by first grade, second grade, third grade on through the high school, and so on through the whole gamut of the present scene. All these matters are subject to change. Administrators should take the lead in discussing them with their respective communities, as many of them are doing and have been doing with good effect. A community is open to reason on these matters. If we don't believe that, we don't believe in man.

The method of administration can make or break the spirit of a school system.

INDEX

Aesthetic values, 180-205; stages of development, 182,3,4; puritanism, 184; art and morality, 185, *see also* Art

Albert Memorial, 52

Americans All, Studies in Intercultural Education (NEA yearbook), 166 n

Appraisal and School Marks (Olson), 149 n

Aristotle, 23, 36, 45, 115

Arts (fine), building attitudes toward, 118; in classroom, 176; Plato on, 187, *see also* Literature; Music

Astronomy (theories of), 201,2,3

Authoritarianism, in Germany, 5; in teaching, 139; Nazi way, 145, *see also* State

Beethoven, 180, 181, 198

Behavior (evaluated), 29; Golden Rule useful principle, 30; conscious, 31; character development, 71; social attitudes affecting, 112; social courtesy, 161, *see also* Morals

Bible, 53

Brown, Dr. S. W. (quoted), 62,3,4; *Secularization of American Education, The,* 63 n

Buddhist faith, 53

Caird, John (quoted), 48; *Introduction to the Philosophy of Religion, An,* 48 n

Church and state, separation of, 6, 8, 9, 98

Christianity, 26, 53, *see also* Hebraic-Christian church; Religion

Civil War (U.S.), 88

Clifford, W. K. (quoted), 103; *Lectures and Essays,* 103 n

Coleridge, Samuel Taylor, *Rime of the Ancient Mariner,* 194

Community, spiritual values in, 10-27; (defined), 11, 12, 17, 26; community living, 49

Comparative religion, 53

Compulsion, no part of appreciation, 111; danger of in teaching, 118,9

Copernicus (theory of), 202,3

Constitution of United States, 72, 98

Declaration of Independence, 51, 74

Democracy (defined), 43, 73; and school, 60; secular pattern of, 75; social, 76; freedom in, 99; compulsion in, 111; in school, 121; respect for individual, 125; group life, 126; democratic schools, 141; part played by teacher in, 143; in school administration, 206,7; social, control in, 212

Democracy and Education (Dewey), 26 n

Dewey, John (quoted), 26, 34; *Experience and Nature,* 34 n; (quoted), 100, 109; *Human Nature and Conduct,* 109 n; (quoted), 182, 188

Dewey, The John Dewey Society, 59

Dialogues, The (Plato), (trans. by Jowett), 87 n

Drake, Charles A., ref. to, 149; *Why Students Cheat,* 149 n